The Remarkable Howe Caverns
Story

The King's Corridor.

The Remarkable Howe Caverns Story

Dana D. Cudmore

THE OVERLOOK PRESS
WOODSTOCK & NEW YORK

First published in paperback in the United States in 2002 by
The Overlook Press, Peter Mayer Publishers, Inc.
Woodstock & New York

Woodstock:
One Overlook Drive
Woodstock, NY 12498
www.overlookpress.com
[for individual orders, bulk and special sales, contact our Woodstock office]

New York:
141 Wooster Street
New York, NY 10012

Library of Congress Cataloging-in-Publication Data

Cudmore, Dana.
The Remarkable Howe Caverns Story / Dana Cudmore.
p. cm.
Includes bibliographical references.
1. Howe Caverns (N.Y.)–History.   2. Howes Cave (N.Y.)–History.
3. Tourist trade–New York (State)–Howes
Cave–History. I. Title
F129.H75C83   1990   89-23014   974.7'45–dc20

Manufactured in the United States of America

ISBN: 0-87951-387-X (hc)
ISBN: 1-58567-246-7 (pbk)

This book is dedicated with all my love to my wife, Nancy, who has endured many years of stories about Howe Caverns and my years as a tour guide there, and to my daughters, Shaun, Libby, Hilary, and Laura.

The book is also dedicated to the staff of Howe Caverns, past, present, and future.

·ENTRANCE·

A Rare Photograph of Old Howe's Cave—Never before published, this scene was taken by a photographer in the last decade of the 19th century. It shows the original entrance to the caverns— an area since destroyed by cement quarrying.
(Photo courtesy of Bob Addis)

Acknowledgments:

This work is a compilation of the author's own research and the numerous articles about Howe Caverns and the caves of Schoharie County that have appeared in book, newspaper, magazine, brochure, and speciality publication form.

The author is deeply indebted to the following: Robert Holt, of the Howe Caverns management, for providing access to the caverns' historical archives and many of the original photographs; Harrison Terk, general manager, for permission to go beyond the "fat man's misery" section of the cave; former Caverns employees Horace Rickard and George Smith, for reminiscing; Robert Addis and Gordon Smith, for additional historical materials from their private collections; John F. Meenehen, who helped research the methods of early cave photography; Warren Howe, for his assistance with the Howe genealogy; Jim Poole, at the *Cobleskill Times-Journal*, for access to newspaper editions covering the years 1926 to 1931; the Schoharie County Historical Society at the Old Stone Fort Museum, Helene Farrell, curator; Timothy Holmes, of the Cobleskill Village Library; and all who in any way over the years have contributed to the body of literature on Howe's Cave.

Contents

Introduction

**HOWE CAVERNS' PLACE
AMONG AMERICAN CAVES
PAST AND PRESENT; ITS
HISTORY PARALLELS THE
INDUSTRIAL AGE.**

Certain places extend the spell of
their glory to the uttermost parts of
the earth, and a long procession of
fascinated pilgrims ever wends its
way to such world-renowned shrines.
One of these is Howe Caverns, made
glorious by the magic of unknown
ages.
—From *The Story of Howe Caverns*,
1936

This history is the most complete yet compiled of
the famous and fascinating cavern. To a great degree,
the story of the popular tourist cave in upstate New York
closely parallels trends in nineteenth- and early twentieth-
century America. The story of Howe Caverns, which was

discovered twenty years before the outbreak of the Civil War, follows America's transformation from a farm-based economy to an industrial nation. It was a time when great fortunes were made by leaders of the Industrial Revolution, and an emerging modern man was eager to exert his command over Mother Nature.

There are 300 or more commercial caves in the United States, but Mammoth Cave of Kentucky, Carlsbad Caverns of New Mexico, Luray Caverns in Virginia's Shenandoah Valley, and Howe Caverns are far and away the most heavily visited. Howe's Cave, as it was then known, was opened for tourists in 1842. It was America's third great commercial cave. Virginia's Weyer's Cave—now Grand Caverns—took in paying customers as early as 1806. Mammoth opened in the mid-1830s; Luray in 1875. Carlsbad, regarded by many as America's most beautiful cave, didn't go commercial until the mid-1920s. That these attractions continue to draw hundreds of thousands of paying vacationers each year is a testament to both their natural appeal and their owners' sharp business sense. Profitability is especially relevant—and impressive—in the case of both Howe and Luray caverns, which are privately owned. (Mammoth Cave and Carlsbad Caverns are run by the National Parks Service.) In 1927, when plans were being made for the revitalization of Howe's Cave, its developers astutely noted that fully one-quarter of the population of the United States lived within only one day's drive of the caverns.

What makes Howe Caverns unique? Though its size is dwarfed by the more than 150 miles of the world's longest cave, Mammoth Cave, and its rock formations are less abundant that Carlsbad or Luray, Howe Caverns boasts what is probably the most remarkable history of any American cave.

Taking the one-hour-and-twenty-minute Howe Caverns tour today, one has a difficult time imagining the way it once was: a muddy, strenuous, all-day expedition lit by crude oil lanterns, and yet gladly patronized by the curious, well-to-do vacationers of the mid-1800s. It is equally difficult to imagine the gargantuan efforts undertaken over the years to develop the caverns for the touring public, to transform them into what we see today.

The story of Howe Caverns is not widely known, and undeservedly so. In the more than 150 years in which Howe Caverns has been a commercial operation, it has had a profound effect on the lives of the explorers, developers, and tourists associated with it, as well as on the small community in which the cave is found. Lives have been lost; fortunes have been created and destroyed; bitter rivalries have developed while competing for the tourist dollar. A modern-day folktale has even evolved, telling of a legendary and hidden cavern, "bigger and better" than the existing one!

It is this fascinating human drama behind the discovery, exploitation, demise, and resurrection of Howe Caverns that earns the cave a unique position in the history of American caves.

Editor's note: In the historical records, Howe Caverns, Howe's Cave, and Howe Cave are often used interchangeably. Until 1927, Howe Caverns was Howe's Cave, named for its discoverer. Howe Caverns is now the official name, given by the corporation that successfully developed the cave and continues its operation. The corporation is Howe Caverns, Inc. Howes Cave (with no apostrophe) is the name of the small hamlet that sprang up around the caverns' entrance and cement works.

2

Earliest Records

A SHORT HISTORY OF THE SCHO-
HARIE VALLEY; INDIAN LEGENDS
AND REVOLUTIONARY WAR HIDE-
OUT; THE STORY BEHIND LESTER
HOWE'S 1842 DISCOVERY.

Howe Caverns winds for nearly a mile beneath the gentle hills of rural Schoharie County in New York's "Leatherstocking region," a name derived from the protective leather leggings worn by sixteenth-century pioneers. The phrase was made famous in the classic works *The Last of the Mohicans* and *The Deerslayer*, by America's first novelist, James Fenimore Cooper. To the east is the Hudson River Valley; to the south lie the foothills of the Catskill mountains; to the north and west is the historic Mohawk Valley. The leatherstocking region is one of the most picturesque areas of New York state. In terms of geology, Schoharie County is the northeasternmost point of a great "cave belt," a geological remnant of an ancient ocean bed that arcs south along the Appalachian Mountains, through

Pennsylvania, the Virginias, Kentucky, and Tennessee, and westward.

Today, the tour guides at Howe Caverns tell the conventional story of the caverns' discovery in 1842 by Lester Howe, a Schoharie County farmer. But the actual discovery took place more than a century before, and the Schoharie valley was rich in history when Howe first entered the cavern that still bears his name.

One hundred and fifty families of refugees from the Palatinate area of Germany settled the area in the early spring of 1713, after two days' journey along an Indian foot trail from the settlement at Albany and over the high Heldebergs. The Indians, a tribe of about two thousand mixed-breeds recognized by the bear insignia of the Mohawk clans, had preceded them by not many years. The valley through which the Schoharie river flows was a paradise for the first white settlers, who located in seven camps, or "dorfs," along the river banks. Though not without hardship, the area was well established at the outbreak of British and Indian hostilities. Its precarious position as New York's westernmost border in the Mohawk Valley led to considerable bloodshed.

The area's caves (of which there are between 150 and 200) are noted in the earliest historical records. For example, the Schoharie Committee of Safety—a six-member organization responsible for revolutionary wartime provisions—held secret meetings in what was called the "committee hole," near Middleburgh. In the 1845 *History of Schoharie County and Border Wars*, author Jeptha R. Simms quotes from the papers of Judge Peter Swart:

"In August, 1777 . . . I was one of six councillors that went from the stone house across Schoharie Creek into the

woods in a cave, to consult what measures to adopt—
secrecy at that time was the best policy."

Simms describes the cave as being on the opposite side
of the river from Middleburgh, in a ravine between the
mountains. The stone house Swart describes was known
as Fort Defyance.

There is also speculation that Ball's Cave, on the hills
high above the Village of Schoharie and county seat, was
once a Tory rendezvous. Peter Ball, the landowner for
whom the cave was named, was chairman of the Committee of Safety.

Prior to the arrival of the German settlers, the Indians
knew of what is now Howe's Cave as "Otsgaragee," or
"Cave of the Great Galleries." In the historical records,
there is some disagreement as to this translation, which
suggests that the Indians explored deep into the cavern.
Naturalist E. George Squier visited the cave in 1842 and
reported: "Human bones as well as pieces of charcoal,
encrusted with a solid coating of carbonate of lime of two
to three inches in thickness have been found at the distance of more than a mile from the entrance." As this
report cannot be verified, the second translation, "Great
Valley Cave," may be the most accurate. A third translation is "Hemp Hill," an Indian reference to the area
around East Cobleskill.

The first white man to enter what is now Howe's Cave
did so in the early 1770s. Perhaps he had been calling on
families in the mill town of Kobel's Kill (today, Cobleskill),
when Jonathan Schmul, a Jewish peddler, sought refuge
from Indian attack by hiding at the entrance to the cave.

Schmul's story was recorded firsthand by the colorful
"Forest Parson," the Reverend John Peter Resig, and first
published in Germany. Resig founded a German Evangeli-

cal Church on the Schoharie, and kept a diary, which today stands as a great historical record of the period. According to the diary, the peddler Schmul was "well informed in matters pertaining to the strained relations" between the Indians, British, and colonists, and took Pastor Resig into his confidence. Upon being asked where he lived, Schmul answered: "I have revealed that to no one, but since you are a minister and can keep the secrets of the confessional, I'll tell you. Ten miles west is a creek named after the German, Kobel, that is Kobelscreek. There I found a cave when the Indians were after me. That's my home. But be mum about this. Should war break out, then flee to this cave and you will be safe." Later, Resig was called upon to visit a sick woman who lay by candlelight in the dimly lit cave.

The diary also describes Resig's Revolutionary War exploits. He once left the cave and "hastened to the scene of the conflict at Oriskany, arriving just as Chief Brant pointed out General Herkimer to the Indians, who made a dash for him." The heroic pastor sprang to the general's side and seized a battle ax in his defense.

Schmul and Resig vanish quite suddenly from the historical records, as did the Indians of the Schoharie Valley, who fled the area with their Tory counterparts at the end of the Revolution. By the time Lester Howe settled in the valley east of Cobleskill, there was little known or remembered of Otsgaragee. The location of the entrance was lost to history. But there was talk of a mysterious "blowing rock"—a strange rocky ledge from which a cool breeze of air emanated on even the hottest days—"so cold and strong, that in summer it chilled the hunter as he passed near it," according to an April 1857 account in *The National Magazine*. "No person ventured to remove the underbrush and rubbish that obscured the entrance, lest some hobgoblin, wild beast, or 'airy creature of the elements,' should pounce upon him as its legal prey."

There was great, yet primitive, interest in the natural sciences in the early 1800s, and in the Schoharie Valley a spontaneous wave of cave exploration took place during the years 1830–1850. Speculation suggests that this interest and exploration can be traced, in part, to the cave explorations in the frontier country of Kentucky, much publicized by the newspapers of the day. Shortly after the War of 1812, the mummified remains of prehistoric Indian explorers were found in Mammoth Cave. Soon thereafter a profitable attraction was established to meet the demands of a curious paying public.

A small group of naturalists and geologists discovered and explored a number of caves in Schoharie County. Some were plundered for their unique mineral formations. In 1831, Gebhard's Cave (previously Ball's' Cave, and now known as Gage's Cavern) was explored, mapped, and made famous by the newspaper writers of the day, notably E. F. yates, a correspondent for the *New York Commercial*. Other cave explorations followed.

T. N. McFail, a professor at the seminary school in Carlisle, explored many of the area's caves. In 1853, McFail died in a fall while climbing from a cave that today bears his name. One "old-timer" with an interest in cave explorations wrote:

"The last climb was too much for him. Professor McFail, I might explain, was exceptionally large. It was finally decided, after several unsuccessful attempts, to tie a loop in a second rope into which he could place one foot. He was able to pull himself up, and his companions were to keep this second rope tight so that he could rest. . . . In this manner, he slowly made his way up until his hat showed above the edge. Then, of a sudden, the weight was gone from the rope and a dull thud came from the bottom.

"According to native lore, his fine gold watch and silk scarf were never recovered."

It is likely Howe was familiar with these explorations and possibly took part in some. His family, including three brothers and two sisters, had settled in the nearby Otsego County community of Worcester at the turn of the century. Howe's grandfather Elijah, as a military man and town tax collector, was pitted against his neighbors in Belchertown, Massachusetts, during the antirent rebellion led by Daniel Shay. It is likely that public opinion forced the Howes to leave their home in Belchertown for upstate New York.

Lester Howe was born January 7, 1810, in Decatur in Otsego County, the second of six children born to Ezekiel and Nancy Howe.

In 1842, at the time of celebrated discovery, Howe and his wife, Lucinda (Rowley) Howe, and their three infant children—Huldah, Harriet, and Halsey John—were a young farm family, having recently settled property in East Cobleskill, adjacent to the caverns' hidden entrance. The property had been purchased by Howe's father from Lucinda's brother, Julius. The farm home faced north from the southern slope of a mile-wide valley, forged by the great glaciers eons ago, through which the Cobleskill Creek wound its way.

The Howe family's farm was equidistant from the villages of Cobleskill and Schoharie, the county seat. Hops, used medicinally and for flavoring beer, was the area's most important cash crop of the early 1800s. Like their neighbors, the Howes probably had a hop house for storing and curing and kept a few cows for milk and butter.

There is no doubt Howe found alluring the story of the strange local phenomenon "the blowing rock." Reports placed its location just north of the "Kobles Kill" and ten miles west of the Schoharie River—on or near his property.

There are several different accounts of the caverns' discovery. The most often-told, simplified for the touring public, is that Howe found the cave on his property by accident. His dairy herd milled about near the cave's hidden entrance to feel the cool air coming from below. (There is probably some element of truth in this aspect of the story; modern-day bovines frequently enjoy the cool breeze from tiny Young's Cave, just north of Howe.) In particular, for many years, a cow named "Millicent" was given credit for helping with the discovery.

Howe's own story even changes over the years. An 1880 promotional account provides the following:

"Howe's Cave was discovered by Lester Howe, whose name it bears, a Schoharie County farmer, who still lives in the vicinity. Howe's own account of the discovery is as follows: While rabbit hunting one day in the fields over this cave, he fell into a "sink hole." Relating this adventure to a scientific man he was informed that sink-holes mark the course of extinct or existing caves. He had also noticed that on hot summer days the cows that were pastured in a field at the present mouth of the cave, were accustomed to huddle together in a certain spot that was in reality less shaded than other parts of the field. But the most singular circumstance was the fact that the temperature in this particular portion was very much cooler than the general temperature. Howe now began to believe that his farm contained a cavern. On the 22d of May, 1842, he and some friends were fox hunting. The fox secreted himself in the face of the hill where the entrance to the cave is to-day. In digging the animal out the cave was discovered."

Whatever his reasons, throughout 1841 and the early months of the following year, Howe was actively looking for a cave or caves. The historical records are agreed on the date: on May 22, 1842, Howe entered the blowing rock after discovering its location on the adjacent property of Henry Wetsel. His neighbor probably accompanied him.

Much to the concern of his wife, Howe, "with commendable curiosity," returned to his discovery day after day, often with Wetsel. There is no firsthand account of Howe's first explorations. He and Wetsel ventured a little farther into the cave on each trip, and emerged wet, muddy, and exalted by the thrill of their discoveries. A piece of tin was hammered into a lamp to burn whale oil, creating for the explorers an easily carried and reliable source of light. Shaped like an inverted funnel, this meager source of light featured a unique tin collar, fashioned to protect the wick from the damp caverns' elements.

Even in its most natural state, Howe's Cave had a grandeur all its own. It is totally unlike almost all other northeastern caves, which require a considerable amount of physical exertion—crawling, climbing, and squeezing through tight, tortuous passages. Howe's Cave consists mostly of walking passages and large rooms, 15 to 30 feet wide, 10 to 60 feet high. A crystal stream of 42-degree water flows through the cavern throughout most of its 1¼-mile course.

But entirely remote from any hint of daylight, caves

exist in utter darkness. The gray limestone walls swallow even the most powerful of lights. Led by a flickering oil lamp not much brighter than a candle, Howe and Wetsel's explorations lasted eight, ten, and twelve hours, and possibly longer. The low, narrow entranceway, filled with beautiful, all-white rock formations—stalactites and stalagmites—led to a wide, airy chamber, later named the "Lecture Room." All about them were broken fragments of the caverns' ceiling, tremendous blocks of limestone rubble, which in places nearly filled the passageway. In a cave, the danger of a cave-in is always more imagined than real, yet the effect is frightening. A visitor in 1861 wrote:

"Never in my life have I seen such rocks—sometimes piles of one above another, and seemingly ready to fall at a touch, and now grand boulders of immense size pushing out from the walls and almost 40 feet above our heads."

As the explorers left the Lecture Room, the light of their lamps was lost in the high-domed ceiling, which shot 60 feet up into impenetrable darkness. The passage split into parallel paths, two grandiose tunnels each about 600 feet long, about 10 feet wide, and between 10 and 30 feet in height. The explorers discovered the passages rejoined, and they entered another large chamber, later named the "Giant's Chapel." Howe and Wetsel had been in the caverns more than two hours at this point, and had traveled only about 1,000 feet. They rested in the chapel, a large room about 40 feet wide by 40 feet long by 60 feet high.

It is at this point that an underground brook crosses the main cave passage, and Howe and Wetsel continued upstream. A later explorer would write romantically:

"Our path . . . was by the side of a little stream of clear, cold water, and before we had gone half a mile we could hear its babble and its dash, which seemed to gather volume as it approached and broke at length upon our ears like the voices of many waters. We crossed the stream I should think a hundred times. Sometimes it was in a chasm below us, then spread out across our path, then babbling merrily at our side—its far off rush the while sounded as if cataracts and waterfalls were plunging into some abyss together. A stream of water underground whose source no one knows!"

Beyond the Giant's Chapel, there were several small side passages heading off the main passage to entice the explorers. Poking and probing the small openings, they discovered another curiosity, and later named this section the Cataract Hall. "There is a small opening in one side which extends far into the mountains," an early visitor wrote. "You put your ear down and listen there and you are astonished and start back. You listen again, and you hear the sound of a cataract pouring over rocks, and you listen till you are filled with awe. There far off in the mountain, where man never was or ever can be, where the Creator's hand and power alone has been, goes down some grand waterfall, just as in the beginning He made it to go, and not the sight of which, but only the sound thereof man is permitted to enjoy."

Howe and Wetsel continued for only about another 600 feet before being stopped at the head of a crystal-clear underground lake. They were unable to cross but could see the cave continued beyond the lake into the blackness. They retraced their footprints in the mud to the entrance and the surface, determined to return.

Materials and tools to build a raft were hauled into the

cave, piece by piece. At the lake's edge, the explorers assembled a crude wooden raft to float them across an underground lake of unknown distance and depth. Leaving the shoreline, Howe and Wetsel knew that if they capsized, they would be without light for many hours—possibly days—before rescuers would arrive. They also risked death from exposure if they became stranded for too long in the damp, cool air, with their clothes soaked in the 42-degree water.

The raft carried the explorers an eighth of a mile to the far edge of the lake. Beyond the lake the discoveries came in quick succession, into great halls and chambers—the most beautiful in the caverns. They climbed over high underground mountains of breakdown—collapsed slabs of the limestone ceiling—and through narrow water-filled canyons. On each trip the explorers made, the cave became more familiar and less foreboding. Eventually, they explored nearly a mile and a half of underground passageway, all by the dim, flickering light of a small oil lamp.

"Improvements" in the cave began almost immediately, and Howe's own announcements to the press heralded the find as "a rival to the great Mammoth Cave of Kentucky."

Yates, the newspaper man who had explored Ball's Cave, returned to the Schoharie Valley to visit the new cavern discovered by Howe. A portion of his report was picked up by the *Supplement to the Courant*, a features-oriented broadside published every other week for subscribers to the Hartford, Connecticut *Courant*.

On Saturday, September 17, 1843, a small headline announced: "A New Natural Phenomenon. Discovery of a vast cavern in Schoharie, N.Y." The *Courant* reported:

"This new cave is not to be identified with the celebrated 'Ball's Cave of Schoharie,' but is reported as far exceeding it in vastness, besides being more remarkable in its structure. Mr. Yates, a correspondent of the New York Commercial, in a long letter of nearly two columns, and from which we make a few extracts, minutely describes this last discovered cavern. It is situated in a northeasterly direction from the Schoharie mountains, near the 'Cave House' kept by Mr. Lester Howe, a very respectable farmer, who is proud of the cave, being for all that is known to the contrary, its discoverer. Mr. Howe entered it for the first time last May, since which, he has made numerous explorations, generating on one occasion, a distance of five miles, and yet not coming to a termination!

No name has been given as yet to the cave, but the letter writer remarks: 'It might not inappropriately be called The Great Tunnel Cave, but the term Gallery, the primary meaning of which is—A long apartment leading to other rooms—is very expressive. Some would perhaps prefer the name Cataract Cave, as the cataract is truly one of its distinguished features.'"

The publication of *Geology of New York*, also in 1843, gave widespread publicity to Howe's find and published the only known rendering of the cavern's original, or natural, entrance. The printers' woodcut shows a much-cleared opening in the limestone hillside, which has since been destroyed.

By the end of the year, Howe and Wetsel had cleared the property near the entrance and cleared mud, clay, and stone from the cave's stream passage to make it more easily traversed. From a report published near the turn of the century, we find an example of Howe's inventiveness:

"A . . . subterranean river was the agent that made the cavern; but it had afterward obstructed it [the entrance] with debris.

"Mr. Howe hit on an ingenious plan for utilizing the water. He first loosened the clay, gravel, and broken rocks; then stopping other outlets he flooded the main channel, and thus forced the stream to sweep out its own deposits."

Howe purchased the property from Wetsel in February 1843, reportedly for $100. The land records use the name "Howe's Cataract Cave" in the description of the transaction.

At age thirty-three, Lester Howe opened Howe's Cave as the country's third commercial cave venture. What became of Henry Wetsel is not part of the historical record, and Wetsel is rarely mentioned in any connection with Howe Caverns. Nearby, Wetsel Hollow Road still winds its way from his former property, over the hill to the village of Schoharie.

EIGHT HOURS UNDERGROUND

The earliest paid explorations through Howe's Cave were real adventures. Howe charged fifty cents—the equivalent today of about $12—to take early adventurers on a torch-lit, 8- to 10-hour caverns tour, through such fancifully named chambers as the "Washington Hall," "Cataract Hall," "Music Hall," and "Congress Hall"; over "Jehosephat's Valley," up the "Rocky Mountains," through the "Fat Man's Misery," and down "The Devil's Gangway."

Often to their chagrin and/or amusement, visitors were

provided with clothing suitable for the caverns trip through mud, clay, and 42-degree water.

A party of four romantically inclined young men and women from the nearby Catskills toured the cave in the late 1800s, and described the attire in the September 7, 1888 issue of the *Dairyman*:

"Everyone carried a lantern and wore a look of determination. It was not considered necessary to add to the attractiveness of the gentlemen. They were provided with straw hats, cow-hide shoes, ungainly overalls and blouses.

"The ladies formed a blooming spectacle in navy blue flannel suits, cut after the most approved pattern and trimmed with white braid. Their costume is best described by saying that it was perfectly adapted to the slippery paths and rugged climbing which the cave affords."

Then, as now, the highlight of the tour was an eighth-of-a-mile boatride across a crystal clear underground lake. At the end of the lake, a unique column of rock formations—formed of both stalactites and stalagmites—produces an eerie, melodious tone when struck. Howe called it "The Harp," and visitors were awed by it and the other wonders in Howe's underground world.

From an historical perspective, it is understandable that after an eight-hour tour the cavern's dimensions would be greatly exaggerated by visitors. Many wrote that the "rival of Mammoth Cave" was at least seven miles in length.

It is also understandable that many thought Howe to be a little bit odd. "An eccentric farmer," an appellation given him by more than one newspaper reporter of the period, appears to have stuck, and does so to this day.

Considering the magnitude of his discovery and its publicity, we know little about the life of Lester Howe. Throughout his life, he displayed the traditional Yankee traits of foresight, ingenuity, inventiveness, and stubbornness. Howe was tall and thin and was considered handsome, if somewhat somber in appearance. He had piercing eyes and a steely glance, with a small mouth partially hidden by a full goatee and mustache. His ears and forehead were prominent, his nose and cheekbones straight and sharp.

In 1851, Simeon North wrote of Howe: "Out of his cave he was awkward and uneasy, like a sailor on pavements; but no sooner were its rocky walls about him than he straightened into a commanding presence."

In the same account, published in *The Knickerbocker Magazine*, North added, "We could now help ourselves to a reason why his chin was badly neglected [a reference to Howe's beard]; why his eyes glared so strangely in the dismal lamp-light; why his back was so partial to a sordid garment. It was that he might impersonate the Stygian ferryman, so as to fill out the description of Virgil: 'His eyes are flames; A dirty robe hangs from his shoulders.'"

The combination of mystery, danger, and the formidable Howe was undoubtedly awe-inspiring, if not on occasion downright frightening. From an April 1857 account:

"On entering the cave we had passed the tunnel of stones thinly covered with water; now the stream had risen so high that there was only a foot of space between its surface and the floor of the passage....

Howe drew near, and so held his lamp that we could clearly see the torrent rushing through the tunnel. 'There,' said he. 'We must either wade through that passage or retrace our steps, and pass the night within the cave.' The water was fast rising, and in twenty minutes would fill the tunnel."

* * *

On another occasion in the cave, Howe "the thunderer" had "petrified his guests into speechlessness." Then, from under his arm, "brought a mysterious box, shaped like a baby's coffin, from which he took out a violin." Howe, the fiddler, made the caverns' visitors "caper about him in wild excitement; his music went to the heels, and the magic of the place transformed his humble instrument into something divine. . . . Our spirits [were] buoyed by the music."

3

The Rival of
Mammoth Cave

THE RIVAL OF MAMMOTH CAVE;
LED BY TORCHLIGHT, TOURISTS
SPEND EIGHT HOURS UNDER-
GROUND; "PIP'S" JOURNAL.

Despite the rigors of the daylong caverns trip by torchlight, Howe's Cave, in the remote hills of Schoharie County, became an overnight success. By 1845, the Howe family's small wood-frame "Cave House" had an addition built on to it to accommodate the growing number of guests.

A decade later, a writer for *The National Magazine* recorded some of his first impressions:

"The traveler is very glad to see a rude gate having 'Howe's Cave' painted in great letters upon one of its bars, and still more glad, when, having turned aside from the main road and crossed a little strip of more smiling landscape, he alights at the door of the hotel, and receives the friendly hospitalities of the great cave explorer."

Travelers would write their impressions of their visit to Howe's Cave in the hotel's guest log, *The Cave Register*. The register has been preserved by the Schoharie County Historical Society.

Students from Union College, in Schenectady, described their tour of May 28, 1849:

". . . entered the Cave with Mr. Howe precisely at Midnight. . . . Two of the party . . . ascended to the top of the ladder in the Rotunda, and each fired off a Roman candle. . . . The party reached the mouth of the cave at 7 o'clock next morning."

Some of the visitor's reactions were written in verse, such as that written October 10, 1852, by an unknown tourist:

> "I have been in the Cave, well what of that
> I've put on the breeches and a dirty old hat
> I've groped lamp in hand as far as one can
> And come out a wiser and dirtier man."

Warren Howe (a distant relative) writes that "visitors seemed unanimous in their appreciation of Lester Howe for his personally guided tours."

The following comments of June 16, 1848, are typical:

"We had hoped after coming out of the Cave to give some sort of sketch but it beggars all description. All we can do is return our sincere thanks to Mr. Howe who conducted us in our journey of five hours to the Rotunda in the very best manner. The reader may rest assured that the visit is every way worthy of the time, expense and trouble."

Lester Howe apparently had a great sense of drama and showmanship. In the caverns' farthest point from the entrance, Howe would fire roman candles up into the high, circular dome called the Rotunda:

"Threw a blazing fire-rocket,—up, up it went, far out of sight, with a convulsive and appalling noise as if a comet had struck the earth and hurled it down from its sphere, dashing and rending it to fragments; and when gravity brought it again to our feet it had no appearance of having reached the top, for the stick or tail was whole, and the rocket itself unbattered. Truly this funnel must reach to an exceeding height."

—from Supplement to the *Courant*, August 22, 1846.

On that same tour, the writer also reported: "Mr. Howe gave several blasts upon a tin horn, the sound of which reverberated along the galleries to the cavern, and echo answering echo through the continuous vaults produced feelings that baffle description. 'Twas [as] if a thousand mad bulls were suddenly let loose around you, roaring, bellowing, and defying each other to the combat."

Howe also used publicity well. Robert Addis, an avid cave explorer and Howe Caverns guide in the 1960s, has what is believed to be the oldest advertising flier still in existence from the heyday of old Howe's Cave. Dated July 1, 1855, it is signed "L. Howe, Proprietor." The text is reprinted here:

HOWE'S CAVE

To the lovers of the wonderful and mysterious in nature, this mammoth Cave, second only to the giant Kentuckian, offers greater inducements than any other place or section of the country that can be found within the wide spreading limits of the American continent. Language is altogether inadequate to portray the thousands of curious objects and singular formations that are constantly presenting themselves to the traveler, as he journeys along through the seven miles of the main thoroughfare of this vast interior of the earth.

During the twelve years this cave has been open to the public, many of the most scientific men of Europe and this country have availed themselves of a personal inspection of the same; have written and lectured upon it, and all agree in pronouncing it one of the greatest natural curiosities to be found in the world.

Every year since the period alluded to, vast sums of money have been expended in clearing and widening the more difficult passages, so that now, ladies can pass through the entire length of the cave with as much facility as a gentleman, and in nearly every instance they seem to take greater delight in performing the journey than their companions of the opposite sex.

The cave is now in excellent order, and visitors may depend upon being conducted through by faithful and intelligent guides; persons who have a personal interest in promoting the prosperity of the undertaking, and making it a place of resort during the summer months, from every part of the United States.

Good and ample accommodations are provided for parties at prices that cannot but be satisfactory.

From Albany to Schoharie the distance is thirty-one miles of excellent plank road, over which passengers are conveyed daily by one of the best stage lines in the country.

Private carriages can be obtained at the latter place, from whence it is but five miles to the Cave, over a pleasant road.

Only a few accounts of the early tours have survived, and it is difficult to reconstruct the entire daylong adventure through Howe's Cave in the mid- to late-1800s.

Shortly after the start of the Civil War, during the summer of 1861, a vacationer whom we can identify only as "Pip" toured Howe's Cave. Addis has information that suggests that Pip may have been young J. Pierpont Morgan, the millionaire banker and philanthropist. Pip was Morgan's childhood nickname, although one of which he was not fond, and it was used only among family. The great banker's estate confirmed Addis's inquiries that Morgan, who would then have been twenty-four, traveled in upstate New York at the time of "Pip's Travel Log."

At the time of Pip's visit, Howe, then fifty-three, had been in business for nearly twenty years. After eight hours in the cave, it is understandable that Pip's descriptions of the cavern's proportions are greatly exaggerated. Yet the account stands as the most comprehensive description we have of Howe's Cave before its commercial development in the late 1920s.

It is evident that Pip was in awe of the caverns' strange beauty, and he writes of the cave with great reverence. He was less impressed with the caverns' tour guide, whom he and his companions gave the uncomplimentary nickname "Plug." The ensuing match of wits that takes place in the cave is truly humorous. With little exception, the account is published in its entirety.

"Pip's Travel Log" is reprinted in part from "A Brief History of Old Howe's Cave—Or How Lester Won in the

End" by Eric Porteus, of Fort Edward, NY. The article was published in the Spring/Summer, 1977, edition of the *Schoharie County Historical Review*, Vo. XXXXI.

PIP'S TRAVEL LOG

My Dear Friend:

Perhaps you will be interested in an account of my summer vacation in 1861: If so, I shall be happy to relate to you that part of it which is between Monday morning, August 19th and Tuesday morning, August 27th. I will now try to give you as good an idea as I can of Howe's Cave.

The entrance is at the base of a mountain which is covered with woods; it opens into a valley which is almost entirely surrounded by rugged hills, there being but one narrow opening through which a small steam of water runs. Perhaps the seclusion and wildness of the place is one reason why the cave was not discovered earlier. The Hotel is built directly above and over the mouth of the Cave, so we have to descend three pairs of stairs to enter it. The proprietor was not at home, and we had for a guide, in his absence, a young man with a short nose, burnt face, hair closely shingled, pants with pockets capacious enough to hold his hands and arms to his elbows, a hat scrimped in the same measurement, eyes close together, and a wiry little mouth which we saw at once would tell us only as many things as we paid him quarters for. Living so far back in the country he labored under the delusion that everybody else lived in a similar locality, and of consequence was as green and conceited as himself. However, three of us were more than a match for one, blunt and rough as he might be, and we succeeded in obtaining such information as we needed. He showed us into the dressing room where were coats, pants, and hats, which he directed us to put on over our other clothes.

They were made of bedticking, were short and large around, covered with mud and full of holes, and when once on us and the hats added, each thought the others transformed into most forlorn Irishmen of the same stamp in appearance and condition of him who said "he was out of money, out of credit, out of clothes, and in debt." A mirror hung in the room and by standing before it we found we were all in the same predicament, one looking as bad as another. Our guide, who wasn't very choice at all in the use of his words, regarding neither elegance or propriety of speech, said we "looked like the Devil." And I admit that saying we "looked like distress" would be keeping back the truth. While we were dressing, our guide went for lights and brought us small oil lamps about four inches tall with a single wick in each, and which we thought would certainly go out. But "Plug"—the name we gave our guide, said "he knew," and told us to follow him: we obeyed and went down the stairs, and entered the mouth of the cave.

The first room, "Entrance Hall," is 150 feet long, about 30 wide and high enough for a tall man to walk comfortably most of the way. While passing through this Hall, I began to ask questions; and first when the cave was discovered: "In 1842," he replied. "How did it happen to be discovered?" said I. "Well, sir," he replied, "Mr. Howe was hunting for caves and came across this." Queer kind of things to be hunting for I thought, and glanced back at my companions to let Plug thereafter carry on the conversation to suit himself; and he immediately began on the state of the country, and informed us with the utmost nonchalance that "Washington had been taken," which seemed to please my companions, and New tried to inform the young man that event had taken place two weeks previous, which led to a reply from Plug, which also led to some tangled talk on the state of affairs between New and Plug—New however, before it was done, elicited from Plug the fact that in those parts they got their mails *at least once a week*—whereupon I said to New, but meaning my words for Plug who I did not highly esteem, that as they were very much behind the times there in regard to items of news and news in general, that, even if the world should come to an end I thought it doubtful if they heard of it until a week or two after it had happened, and that, as he didn't succeed in making the impression upon a young man's mind which he wished, he had better drop the subject entirely: our coming suddenly to a new spacious hall at once ended our conversation and changed the subject for us. . . .

We were now in Washington Hall, which is 300 feet long, about as wide as Entrance Hall, and a good deal higher, from 40 feet upwards. On entering every room, our guide had some little legend to relate either in regard to its being named, or something which the name might suggest, and these stories he told in a kind of singing voice as if he had told them a hundred times before and knew exactly into what chasm to point or throw his light to make his account as thrilling as possible, and the more thrilling they were, the less he believed them: and our stay in each room I noticed corresponded with the length of his stories. "Old Tunnel" and "Giant's Chapel" were next passed, and in the latter place we had rehearsed some old tale from the Arabian Nights, which either Plug believed had actually happened there, or else, what is more probably, himself didn't know to the contrary.

I may as well state that I was positively afraid to enter the cave. New had visited it before and had now no such fears. Plug noticed my timidity, and in his rehearsals added that in such and such places there was great danger, looking sympathizingly at me always, and the more he added to his stories with a view to increase my alarm, the more bold I became, and after the first mile, felt no sense of danger at all. I would not blame a person for feeling timid at first, for great chasms at your side and massive rocks above stare you in the face and threaten to destroy you, and you can't help believing that they will keep their word.

Our path all the way was by the side of a little stream of clear, cold water, and before we had gone half a mile we could hear its babble and its dash, which seemed to gather volume as it approached and broke at length upon our ears like the voices of many waters. We crossed the stream I should think a hundred times. Sometimes it was in a chasm below us, then spread out across our path, then babbling merrily at our sides—its far off rush the while sounded as if cataracts and waterfalls were plunging into some abyss together. A stream of water underground whose source no one knows! Yet it has a mission, feeding some far off spring perhaps—and always busy at its task with a cheerful happy laugh!

We came next to Harlem Tunnel which is 600 feet long. Frequently on the sides of the rooms were large openings which we did not enter, as most of them had not been much explored. Never in my life have I seen such rocks—sometimes piles of one above another, and seemingly ready to fall at a touch, and now grand boulders of immense size pushing out from the walls and almost 40 feet above our heads, while through the openings between we could gaze upwards but only into the darkness. Perhaps you can get some idea if you will recall how on a hot summer day those terrific thunder clouds roll up from the north and west and sometimes meet; they are dark and threatening, and awful; so those huge rocks that I saw pushing out from either side far above me reminded me of those clouds, and seemed as black and as terrific as they.

We then passed through Cataract Hall, which is 300 feet long and remarkable for this: about midway there is a small opening in one side which extends far into the mountains; it is not known how far, for it cannot be explored. But here is something most curious; for you put your ear down and listen there and you are astonished and start back. You listen again, and you hear the sound of a cataract pouring over rocks, and you listen till you are filled with awe. There far off in the mountain, where man never was or ever can be, where the Creator's hand and power alone has been, goes down some grand waterfall, just as in the beginning He made it to go, and not the sight of which, but only the sound thereof man is permitted to enjoy. I tell, my friend, man begins to feel his littleness in such a place, for all about him are marks of a Power that must have been Almighty. Yet the Hand that opened these chambers, and balanced those stupendous rocks, and marked out the part for the merry brook, and poured the far off invisible Niagara, still keeps them in their primal order.

Then we pass the "Pool of Siloam" where the water bubbles up like a little fountain, and seemed to sparkle with delight as we held our lamps near to it. Then came "Franklin's Hall" where Plug had to repeat the famous saying which old Benjamin gives in one of his letters as the advice of a mother to him when he was quite young. Plug gave it to use in this form—"Then gentlemen I advise you to remember to stoop as you go, and you will miss many hard thumps"—saying it with all the gravity and dignity of gray-headed Mother himself, so that we couldn't help laughing him in the face.

We came next to the "Flood Hall" where the course of Plug must relate how several persons got so far once when the water rose suddenly and they had hardly time to save themselves by flight, and indeed were waist deep in water before they reached the Entrance: adding, of course, as a subject for our contemplation, what we already knew, that there had been a flood a few days before we came, but he thought there was no danger now.

"Congress Hall" had something of interest besides its legend. But in "Music Hall" which follows it, there is so much more of interest that I will omit the former.

And first is the echo, whence the name of the Hall. A small aperture in one side is just wide enough to admit one's head, who makes some audible sound with his voice, and oh what a melody!—as if a thousand harps were struck. It matters not if the sound be ugly, echo calls out to echo, and wave follows wave, till melody is all about you. I could have listened to this music for hours. If my soul was filled with awe in "Cataract Hall," it was here calmed by the sweet voice of music more harmonious than toneful lips or chord or viola or harp.

Editor's Note: At this point, Pip's tour leaves the "historical section" of Howe's Cave, and proceeds through the half mile of cavern which is now seen as part of the commercial tour. Much of the historical section has been destroyed by the quarrying of limestone for cement manufacturing.

Pip's account continues:

The second curiosity of "Music Hall"—and "Musical" is its proper name—is its Lake, of considerable length and from 10 to 30 feet deep. [The underground lake has since been named "The Lake of Venus."] It is one of the most remarkable sights I ever saw. Its waters are clear as crystal and its surface is smooth as glass. Here I saw more of a resemblance to the River of Death than language or fancy ever painted for me. I could hear the dip of muffled oar, and looked upon our guide as a second Charon, taking us over to some unknown shore. We strained our eyes to see across it, but the feeble rays of our lamps could not light up the darkness which hung its thick veil over the far-ther side. We stood perfectly quiet in the boat, and our lamps hove their light over ten thousand stalactites that hung like clusters of icicles from the ceiling and sparkled above us like a starry sky. Huge blocks of limestone were piled up on our right hand and on our left. We heard yet the same confused rush of water as before, but here in the stillness it came with a mellower and sadder sound. Darkness now began to close in behind us, and we seemed to be imprisoned there. We passed slowly on with none but solemn thoughts, and in a little while reached the farther shore.

At the end of the lake is what is called "Annexation Rock" or "Rock of the World's History"; it is a limestone formation of immense size, 20 feet in diameter and 40 feet high. It is egg-shaped—much the largest in the middle. Our guide said these stones form *an eighth of an inch in a century!*

We went then through "The Fat Man's Misery," a low narrow place where those who are slim and short have altogether the advantage.

Then came the "Museum," where all sorts of formations, some the most beautiful ever beheld, both hanging from the ceiling and side formations, which I can describe better after I finish the room. The Museum is one-half mile long.

Then we begin to ascend the "Alps," and here look out for your feet! We seemed to stand man above man, and each clinging to the loosened rocks. The summit is soon reached,—and they are not of very great height, and take their names more from their steepness and roughness, I suppose;—and then came the descent which is as trying and not at all safer, —but we came down perfectly well, and came into the "Bath Room" [probably what is now known as "The Bronze Room," which still shows the sooty residue of early visitors' oil torches] where there is a pool of water and sundry other arrangements from which a vivid imagination, like Plug's for instance, could easily believe this to be the Bath Room of the spirits who inhabit there. It certainly has to recommend it, that it is the most retired Bath Room I ever saw.

Next came "Pirate's Cave," but I doubt if any pirate ever saw it: indeed it seemed to me it would require more of pirate courage to venture so far underground as we were than to go on the most hazardous trip a sea-robber ever made.

We came next to the "Rocky Mountains" [to this day "The Rocky Mountains" and "The Winding Way" still bear the names given them by Lester Howe]; in ascending either these or the Alps and I have forgotten which, we were obliged to go up by ladder a part of the way.

We then passed them safely and came down into "Jehosephat's Valley," one mile in length. [Underground, distances are deceiving: the passage is actually just 80 feet long.] Like the one of old it is a deep ravine with the steep sides, and the brook running at the bottom. It is said of the old Valley that every nook and every available spot is crowded with the graves of Moslems and Jews who think it the greatest honor to be buried there, for each expects that Jehovah or Mohammed will come back to that spot to judge the dead at last.

"Miller's Hall" we passed through next, where we pause a moment to take leave of the brook which has been our companion so long, and also of the Cave proper. There is a dark chasm overhead and a deep ravine below where the Cave and Brook lose themselves; rocks have fallen here so that the Cave cannot be explored beyond.

Here we turn a little to the right and enter what is called "Winding Way," which fully realizes the import of the name. Solid rocks on either side, very close together, very high in some places and low in others, we twist, and bend, and compromise, and turn, and turn, and turn, round and round it seems, for a long distance, yet the turns are so frequent and the formations on the sides so close to our faces, and the stillness is so great, for the rushing of waters has ceased now that we pass the distance pleasantly and rapidly.

We came out into a small room, and I looked down into a dark hole called "The Devil's Gangway"; it is but little larger than a barrel and 30 or 40 feet long, down into which people must go, head foremost, on their hands and knees, and not expect to turn round or back out. Some fat men have been stuck here and have had to do their best to get either one way or the other.

Editor's Note: A previous days' rainfall fills the small passage at this point, and makes it impossible to continue into the final section of the cave. Plug describes the cave for Pip and New, and they sit and rest before starting back. Pip estimates they are now "six or seven miles" from the caverns' entrance.

They retrace their steps to leave the cave, Pip continues his account by describing the formations he has seen:

Let me first mention what is called "Lot's Wife," a formation resembling a human body and of life size. Plug did not know whether it was Lot's first or second wife. . . .

In one place was a church—most perfectly represented—with towers and windows and doors. Nearby was an organ with its long large pipes in the middle, and at the ends shorter ones, and arranged in such perfect order you should think it real.

There were also many kinds of vegetables represented: Here was a bunch of carrots, perfect as if just pulled from a garden: Here a bunch of grass or grain hanging like a sheaf without any band with the heads downward. In another place was a pair of elephant ears, of life size, and in perfection form. Then there was a pair of doves, loving each other as dearly as people pretend doves do. Again we saw sparrows and other birds.

There was also a soldier with his armor on, as if some mythic hero had arrayed himself for battle and by some strange overmastering power was suddenly transfigured and transformed into a pillar of stone— to keep a nightly watch for ages. Not far from here were two women in long flowing robes, facing each other and seemingly engaged in earnest conversation.

But I was most interested in the formation which studded the ceiling above the lake. While the guide was fixing the boat, I ran up the bank to let my lamp shine through them, and also to examine another formation, which, on the whole, was the most curious I saw. My companions were down by the lake, and a growl came up to me from Plug "not to touch that thing," to which I paid no attention whatever, and went on and examined the curiosity to my heart's content. If I had been told that it was a wet skin taken immediately from the tannery and hung there by two or three hooks, so that the folds might hang gracefully, I should have believed it. And now I can think of nothing better unto which to liken it: Imagine a hairless buffalo robe thoroughly wet, and attached to the ceiling of a room by three hooks about six inches apart, and you have as correct an idea as I am able to give you of this formation. Its thickness was uniform; its folds were graceful; and altogether it was the most singular thing I saw. And now imagine the ceiling of a large room studded with icicles so as to describe every conceivable angle and curve, and have them of different lengths and you will get some idea of the number and beauty of the formations which hung over the lake. These limestone formations are not as clear as crystal, and are not transparent— they are a dingy white; but because they are constantly wet, the rays of our lamps were reflected by them, causing them to appear most beautiful.

At the place where the Cave and brook lose themselves I went down into the ravine and drank a good draught of the water which was sweet and pure and cool. . . .

Editor's Note: Closing his letter, Pip writes quite eloquently of a unique feeling, one shared by all cave explorers, past and present:

There is also this singular factor to be noticed, that a person seldom feels fatigued in the cave; but on the contrary they are strong and vigorous and ready for any amount of action; there is an exhilaration of spirits; and a suppleness of strength imparted to one such as is no where on the surface of the earth. But, when one comes out into the open air they are ready to rest, for the exhilarating power is gone and a reaction comes. . . .

If you should have the least pleasure in reading what I have written, I shall be more than rewarded for the little trouble it has cost me to record these events, in knowing that I have done anything, however slight, for your gratification.

Yours Truly,
"Pip"

4

Howe Loses His Cave

"LESTER HOWE...IS NOT A VERY SMART MAN"; CORPORATE MANEUVERINGS AND QUARRY OPERATIONS CLOSE HOWE'S CAVE.

Throughout the 1850s and 1860s, the caverns attracted an increasing number of visitors. Howe's Cave became a prominent tourist attraction, known throughout the nation. In 1847, one newspaper reported that "within 20 miles of Albany, there is a vast cave, far exceeding in its extent and novelty, the Mammoth Cave of Kentucky."

An advertising flier, printed much later, boasted: "This is one of the most remarkable curiosities in the United States. For extent, beauty, and variety of scenery, it is only equaled by the Mammoth Cave...with the advantages of being more convenient of access, and without danger."

Just getting to Howe's Cave, in the remote foothills of Schoharie County, presented difficulties that few modern-day vacationers would endure. Schenectady and Albany, were, and are, the nearest metropolitan areas. Travelers arrived via boat trip along the Hudson or Mohawk river, or by barge along the Erie Canal, the primary water routes of the day. The early rail lines also brought travelers to New York's Capital District. (The iron horse would not reach into Schoharie County until 1869.) It was 31 miles by coach or horse from Albany along the Great Western Turnpike (now U.S. Route 20) to the northernmost point of Schoharie County. From there, dirt ruts and roads led to the Charlotteville Turnpike, the county's main thoroughfare, built of wooden planks laid together in the late 1840s. An uncomfortable carriage ride took travelers the remaining 10 or so miles to the caverns' entrance on the hillside. Yet throughout this period, thousands of visitors each year made the trip to Howe's Cave.

Contributing to the caverns' appeal as a preferred vacation spot was the Howe family's Cave House Hotel. While the challenging, eight-hour cave tour was only for the adventurous, the gracious accommodations of the Cave House could be enjoyed by all.

The first Cave House burned to the ground in 1847. When building its replacement, Howe built the northern wing of the spacious hotel directly above the caverns' entrance. Visitors entered the cave through a stairway in the basement of the building, and cool air from the cave circulated up through the lodge. This innovation provided guests of the Cave House, mostly "city folk," the first form of air conditioning—a rare respite from the summer heat.

The air in the cave was the subject of much scientific inquiry and speculation by the learned men of the day. The news correspondent E. F. Yates wrote: "On emerging from the cave, I noticed, as I had done before, on leaving Ball's cave, the great difference between the air of the cave and of the upper earth." Yates compared the air of the cave to "pure cool water of the living fountain"; the outside air to the "insipid water of the rain-vat." The nitrous earth of the cave, he said, "imparts a healthy action to the respiratory organs, and slightly exhilarates while it invigorates the whole system. As germane to this subject, witness the cures of consumption effected by breathing the fumes of nitric acid, and the experiment of Dr. Mitchell, of Kentucky, who being much debilitated and afflicted with a pulmonary complaint, was restored to health by inhaling for a period the air of the celebrated Mammoth Cave of that state."

Sitting on the northern slope of the valley, the Cave House commanded magnificent views of the countryside. Guests could share pleasant conversation or relax in the early summer evening in the rocking chairs on the hotel porch. The dining rooms were spacious and cheerful, and served delicious meals, prepared from the freshest beef, poultry, and dairy products from the neighboring farms. At night, guests were probably entertained by Howe or one of his daughters at the family piano. Lester was remembered by one elderly gentleman as an accomplished pianist.

Below the hotel, the caverns provided an inexhaustible supply of cool, crystal water. Later owners of the hotel would write, "Although we make no special claim as to its medicinal qualities . . . it has been pronounced by competent persons to possess rare properties, having in a number of known cases produced the most beneficial results."

Howe was regarded as an oddity by his neighbors, and stories of his peculiar behaviors persist to this day. He was referred to in newspaper accounts published as late as the 1930s as "an eccentric genius."

Perhaps the oddest example of Howe's behavior was an 1854 publicity stunt in which he staged his daughter's wedding in the cave. On September 27, Harriet Elgiva Howe wed Hiram Shipman Dewey in a natural loft called the Bridal Chamber just within the caverns' entrance to old Howe's Cave. Ironically, Dewey was a surveyor for the coming railroad, the president of which, Joseph Ramsey, would later take control of the Howe's Cave property.

A century later, one of the couple's descendants recalled: "[Harriet] was small and retiring with blue eyes and an abundance of light brown hair. The groom, whose name is tucked away inconspicuously in a corner of the invitation to the wedding reception, was six feet tall, handsome and fun-loving, with dark brown hair and deep blue eyes."

It is not as widely known that the Howe's eldest daughter, Huldah Ann, was married in the caverns earlier that year, according to Frances Howe Miller, a direct descendant. It would have been the first wedding to take place in a cave anywhere in the country.

Considering the influence of the church on family life in the mid-1800s, the two weddings in the caverns were probably considered near blasphemy. Based on the few stories of Lester Howe's behavior that have been told and retold over more than a century, it seems likely Howe would not have cared.

The Howe-Dewey wedding is a much-publicized part of the caverns' historical record. The bride must have been a very agile young lady: a photo of the wedding in the modern entrance lodge shows her wearing an all-white gown and veil and standing atop a muddy bank in the torchlit cave. And today, Harriet Elgiva's wedding is commemorated daily on the cave tour in the "Bridal Altar."

The couple's first child and the Howes' first grand-daughter, Annie Laurie Dewey, was born to Hiram and Harriet in the family's Cave House Hotel on September 12, 1860. Annie was the first of six children the couple would have.

Another story of Howe's eccentricities is that he had his carriage drawn tandem, with two horses in a single file. Howe's reason for doing so, as the story has been related, is that he only wanted to be different; his neighbors paired their horses side by side.

He once advertised an auction to be held at his property. When the grounds were filled by his neighbors and potential bidders, he brought out his eldest daughter, Huldah, for a piano recital.

An elderly Barnerville resident told this story many years ago to a former manager at the "new" Howe Caverns. As a young boy, he remembered Howe (who was then quite old) pulling up in his carriage to the Barnerville general store. The local minister greeted him, "Good Morning, Lester. I hear the cock do crow; methinks it will rain." To which Howe replied, "I thought God made the weather, Reverend."

From 1851, there was much talk in the Schoharie Valley of establishing a railroad to connect the Albany rail line to the New York and Erie railroad to the southwest. The train would run through the Cobleskill, Schenevus, and Susquehanna valleys, and stock would be subscribed to finance a $6 million construction contract. The coming arrival of the Iron Horse prompted great excitement. Towns along the proposed route, as well as individual subscribers, all purchased shares of rail stock in the new Albany and Susquehanna Railroad.

After several delays, right-of-way conflicts, and legal

entanglements, the Albany and Susquehanna Railroad was completed in 1865. Visitors could arrive and depart from the station established at the hamlet of Howes Cave, an easy two-mile walk or carriage ride from the Cave House Hotel. The number of visitors to the cave increased steadily; Howe Caverns became a leading New York tourist attraction, second only to Niagara Falls. It was perhaps the country's most famous cave.

Howe, then in his late fifties, prospered. He continued to add to his property holdings and make improvements to the cave, seriously overextending himself in the process. In 1869, a small kiln for processing limestone into cement was established a short distance to the south of the cave entrance, along the mountain ridge that had, in part, been carved by the railroad. Howe added property to the venture and joined in partnership. In the cavern, he began to install an expensive experimental system of gas lighting, with pipes extending one-half mile from the hotel entrance to the foot of the underground lake. A flier of the period boasted Howe's Cave as "The Only Cave in the World Lighted by Gas!" (Some of these pipes, corroded with age, still exist. They can be found in the undeveloped portion of Howe Caverns, which today lies beyond the lake.) Along the same trail, he began laying rails and ties for a small, narrow-gauge train ride to carry visitors from the cave entrance to the foot of the lake.

Then, in January 1872, the second Cave House burned. The public's interest in caves waned. The number of visitors had been declining steadily.

To keep his small empire afloat and to finance the construction of a third hotel, Howe entered into a joint-stock agreement with railroad magnate/politician Joseph Ramsey and two other partners. Ramsey, a state senator, was instrumental in bringing the railroad to Howes Cave, and evidently had been watching the Howes' affairs for some time. An astute businessman, the president of the Albany and Susquehanna Railroad realized there was a huge market for cement and plaster as a building material.

In matters of business, Ramsey was not a man to be trifled with. In 1869, Ramsey faced a crucial proxy fight led by prominent rail tycoons Jay Gould and "Diamond" Jim Fisk, of the Erie Railroad. Financial and legal infighting ensued, and Ramsey won.

The business plan of the Howe Cave Association called for substantial capital improvements of the kiln and processing equipment and stepped-up mining efforts in the limestone quarry to meet the new demand. Lester Howe's beloved cave received less attention, although plans called for the construction of a third hotel and improvements to the surrounding property.

According to reports, Ramsey, on several occasions, offered to buy Howe's interest in the cave, but Howe refused. He loved the cavern too deeply. Finally, when Howe was fifty-nine and increasingly eccentric, Ramsey succeeded.

It is difficult to pinpoint exactly when, and how, Ramsey took control of the Howe's Cave property. Warren Howe writes that it probably took place over a number of years, Lester being the victim of "corporate maneuverings he did not fully understand."

The Ramsey organization saw things differently. In a 24-page promotional description of the cave and hotel, the anonymous author writes: "He [Howe] sold it at a high figure to the Howe's Cave Association, its present owners, and then retired to a small farm on the opposite side of the valley, where he still lives in peace and quietness."

From the archive collection of Howe Caverns, Incorporated, comes the following advertisement by the new management, dated April 26, 1869:

"Howe's Cave—Situated on the Albany and Susquehanna Railroad, 39 miles from Albany, N.Y. Trains stop daily. The above named property having passed out of the hands of its former proprietor into the hands of an association, organized under State Laws, the avenues through the Cave have been much improved, without changing natural positions or geological formations, rendering this world renowned subterranean cavern still more accessible than heretofore. The Cave-House, a commodious summer resort for pleasure seekers, has been conveniently arranged, and is ready for the reception of visitors. No pains will be spared to entertain and entirely satisfy the thousands who annually visit these grounds. Experienced guides constantly in attendance to conduct boarders and visitors through the Cave."

Typical of the early industrial period, Ramsey was regarded as a hero of the business age. The event was recorded in the September 11, 1873, edition of *The Daily Graphic*.

"Howe . . . is not a very smart man. That is, he didn't understand joint stock companies. When President Ramsey, of the railroad here, offered Mr. Howe $10,000 for his cave, he refused it; but the next day the good Mr. Ramsey organized a joint stock company, the Howes Cave Company, called the capital stock $100,000, and then paid Mr. Howe $12,000 in stock for his cave. As the cave was all the stock ever paid in, Mr. Ramsey is ahead just $88,000, and Mr. Howe $12,000. This shows power of intellect. It shows how a shrewd, honest businessman can always succeed, while dishonest people fail. The poor farmer now hoes his beans and milks his cows on the barren hills, while Mr. Ramsey smokes his 'Henry Clay' on the balcony of the Cave House. Such is life."

(Later, Ramsey would be instrumental in creating the First National Bank of Cobleskill, now Key Bank, N.A. A century later, Key Bank is now the bank of record for Howe Caverns, Incorporated.)

Howe retired to his property across the valley, a lush plateau on the mountainside he named "The Garden of Eden." From his front porch, he watched train cars of visitors load and unload at the Howes Cave depot, and watched smoke rise from the cement kilns. He became increasingly bitter. Howe lost control of his cave. But he vowed he would have the last laugh on Mr. Ramsey, and on the world.

Cobleskill historian Arthur H. Van Voris researched the following article from a July 1884 edition of the *Cobleskill Herald*. The article was published just four years before Howe's death in 1888 at age sixty-eight. In it, Howe boasts of having discovered a "bigger and better cave." Perhaps it was an act of retribution, or perhaps it was a benign practical joke born of New England wit. With a single haunting statement, Howe created a mystery that remains unsolved to this day. A lost cavern of unparalleled beauty—surely worthy of commercial development.

The Garden of Eden property, as described, no longer exists. The Howes' property, house, and farm buildings had long since been abandoned by the time plans were announced for a major interstate highway in the early 1970s. Today, I-88 connects Binghamton to the Capital District, with four lanes of highway directly above Howe's Garden of Eden farm.

A measure of Howe's state or mind at the time can be

surmised by reading between the lines of the following article. Written fifteen years after his loss of the cave which he made famous, it is apparent that Howe, still bitter, continued to seek ways to entertain the public. In addition to the Garden of Eden cave, the article also describes new "scientific finds" by Howe and announces plans for a hotel, racetrack, and telephone line to the Garden of Eden station.

From the *Cobleskill Herald:*

"The Garden of Eden was about equidistant from Cobleskill and Schoharie, and was reached by taking a turn in the road to the left, near East Cobleskill. . . . One soon reaches a road roofed with overhanging boughs and immense boulders and rocks on the right side, and a beautiful forest on the left. Shortly a clearing of about 20 acres is reached and in this clearing is the famous "Garden of Eden."

"On the north side is located Lester Howe's house and barns on the edge of a deep gorge. The cleared space is surrounded by a fine timber belt through which a carriage driveway extends the whole distance of one and one-half miles. The driveway has never been fully completed.

"The cleared space is so located that the winds sweep over it without touching, and the surrounding hills and forest protect the fruits and crops from the frost. Hence, semi-tropical crops are quite easily produced here and Mr. Howe has 15 acres of fruit trees, including 300 pear, apple, peaches, plums, quince, plus grapes, raspberries, strawberries, blackberries, and currants in profusion.

"Sweet potatoes are successfully grown in quantity

and early frosts which do damage on nearby properties do no damage here.

"The south side of this productive garden is by a
fertile hill, where it is always cool and refreshing.
The trees are tall and straight and furnish excellent
shade. This south side is heavily timbered and fringed
along the top with mossy rocks principally of the
limestone formation, which erosion has produced a
picturesque appearance.

"The fine opportunity for study by geologists has
been taken advantage of as there are numerous recesses
in the rocks where, in the hottest weather, the air is
comfortably cool, so that one can sit within and enjoy
the gorgeous view which extends for miles before the
eyes of the viewer. And along the base of these rocks
there extends a natural and easily traversed path; at
its foot the ground is ideal, and here is a delightful
picnic spot.

"The so-called "Jersey Bed Chamber" is located to
the left of the entrance to the grounds. Here Mr.
Howe has several superior Jersey cows and calves,
which retreat into this grove in hot weather, hence its
name. This area is a charming gulf through which
trickles a silvery stream. In its bed and along its sides
are immense rocks weighing hundreds of tons; all
lovers of nature will be well repaid to gaze upon this
spot.

"Mr. Howe has left it just as it was created by
Nature, not even removing a single branch from the
trees. Velvety moss covers the rocks and logs.

"To the west, the grove extends almost to the
village or hamlet of East Cobleskill; this part is much
higher and is located at the base of the majestic

wooded hill with its splendid view toward Albany and Schenectady.

"The air is bracing and it is here that Lester Howe has surveyed off a one-half mile driving-and-trotting track which will be finished as soon as the crops are harvested. We do not hesitate to state that in no place in the entire state is there a finer view than is afforded from this "Garden of Eden."

"A house on the spot will have an addition built onto it and it will then, according to the owner, be turned into a hotel where weary travelers can rest and be refreshed. Mr. Howe is having a telephone line to Howes Cave village installed, and he is calling his phone station "The Garden of Eden."

"Among the numerous geologic specimens displayed by Mr. Howe, there is one which he found here, greatly resembling a petrified human head. He found it wedged between the rocks in a deep crevice into which he believes, in ages past, a man fell and could not extricate himself. He thinks it could have been one of the Mound Builders. The nose, mouth, eyes, ears, and jaw bone are very plainly defined in this petrified mass. The entire soil seems to rest upon the fossil remains of numerous animals and corals.

"Throughout this Garden of Eden, comprising in all some 75 acres, there are many excavations evidently made in ancient time. Into one of these pits, Mr. Howe came upon a stone 'vault,' which was so recent that he had not yet gotten around to fully investigate its nature, and possible contents.

"Mr. Howe's connection with the Howe Cave project, which cave he, himself, discovered, did not terminate in any satisfactory and profitable manner for him, so he now has no connection with it, whatever.

"Here it is that he purchased acreage known today as The Garden of Eden, and he has frequently stated that he has discovered a 'bigger and better cave.' It is surmised by many that its opening is located somewhere in this territory and it is hoped that one day he will announce to the public and open for inspection his new-found cave, and we wish him and his 'Garden of Eden' the best of luck."

It is interesting to speculate on the impact the caverns had on the Howe family. Howe certainly felt the exuberance of his 1842 discovery. With great pride he prepared the cave for visitors, not only clearing paths where possible but also giving names to the caverns' great hallways and formations, such as "The Music Room," "The Winding Way," and "Annexation Rock." His continued trips into the cave probably caused his wife great concern for his safety, and on occasion his farm chores were probably overlooked while Howe went "cavin'."

In the earliest years, the first visitors to the cave were the naturalists, scientists, writers, and other educated men and women of the period. Howe undoubtedly felt ill at ease—"like a sailor on pavement"—in their presence. Born to a farm family in a rural backwoods area, Howe received no formal education of which there is any record. But Howe's Cave earned for Lester, the "eccentric genius," the respect and admiration of even the most well-educated and well-placed visitor.

Warren Howe writes: "If Lester's loss of ownership [of the cave] bothered him in later years . . . he should not be remembered in this context. Lester's real importance to

HOWES CAVE,

SCHOHARIE CO., N. Y.

Entrance within a few rods of the depot, on
the Albany and Susquehanna Railroad,
39 miles from Albany.

THE ONLY CAVE IN THE WORLD
LIGHTED WITH GAS !

DESCRIPTION OF THE CAVE.

This is one of the most remarkable c
For extent, beauty and variety of scener
moth Cave of Kentucky, with the advan
access, and without danger.

This Cave is Lighted with Gas as far :
one mile. The cavern extends for miles.
ly. The average temperature of the Cav
the entire year. The air is pure and inv

TO EXCURS

Sabbath Schools will find this one of t.
as there is one of the most beautiful grov
with plenty of seats and tables, free to s
on said premises. Sabbath Schools adm
Car rates can be obtained at the Compan
N. Y. Circulars will be furnished free to

A First-Cla
Known as the CAVE HOUSE. has been

For further particulars address

E. HILTS
HOWES CAVE, SCH

AN EARLY ADVERTISEMENT FOR THE CAVE HOUSE HOTEL—Built
above the caverns' entrance, cool air circulating up from the cave
provided welcome relief to visitors on hot summer days. *At
bottom*, THE HOTEL'S ABANDONED REMAINS—The hotel as it looks
today at the edge of Howes Cave Cement Quarry. Chill breezes
still blow up from the original entrance.

Top left, CHAUNCEY RICKARD—A flamboyant, self-educated farm boy, Rickard developed the caverns' modern presentation, drawing heavily on his knowledge of Greek mythology. He was the first tour guide employed by Howe Caverns, Inc. *Above*, JOHN MOSNER—The Syracuse engineer who proposed in 1926 the restoration of Howe's Cave through modern engineering techniques. *At left*, LESTER HOWE, 1810–1888 *(Photos courtesy Howe Caverns, Inc.)*

AFTER THE SHAFT FOR THE CAVERNS' ELEVATOR ENTRANCE was completed, work in the cave progressed more rapidly. A winch, hoist, and bucket took workers down 156 feet to the section of the cave under development. *(Photo courtesy of Howe Caverns, Inc.)*

THE CHINESE PADOGA—An un-
identified explorer with Professor Cook's 1906 survey poses
with the caverns's largest stalagmite, "The Chinese Pagoda."
(Photo courtesy of New York State Museum)

THE ROTUNDA—Early visitors relax and smoke their pipes in the
torchlit Rotunda Room, once the
farthest point from the cave's
original entrance. The Rotunda—
beyond the "Fat Man's Misery"
section of the Winding Way—is
no longer part of the commercial tour. This engraving is from
a series of woodcuts circa 1880.
(Courtesy Howe Caverns, Inc.)

Howe Caverns was not his discovery and one-time ownership, but his exploration, development, and presentation
of that phenomenon to the world. By contrast, what
individual or group achieved ultimate ownership is trivial.
The latter will pass, but Lester Howe's idea and the efforts
he made to make the cave an opportunity for human
wonder, delight, and learning will live on."

For more than twenty-five years from the time of its
discovery, the world-renowned Howe's Cave was, for the
most part, a family business. The Howe family was not
made wealthy by the cave, nor were they left as paupers
by Ramsey's shrewd stock manipulations.

Yet there is some satisfaction in knowing that Ramsey's
ownership of the commercial portion of the caverns' property eventually turned out to be less than profitable.

Before transferring his property to the Howes Cave
Association, Howe had completed the construction of a
third Cave House Hotel. To this imposing gothic structure
of cut limestone, the Ramsey organization built an extensive addition (of wood), which more than doubled its size.
It was renamed the Howes Cave Pavilion Hotel. Spacious
rooms were added for fancy dress balls, billiards, and even
indoor bowling; the lawns were manicured for tennis and
croquet; and a livery stable provided "good vehicles and
horses at reasonable rates."

It is evident that the Ramsey organization felt the resort
business would be more profitable than the cave business.
Lester Howe had charged fifty cents for a tour through his
cave; rates for room and board at the Pavilion Hotel were
$2.50 per day, and $10 to $15 per week. The hotel's
promotional literature was reprinted in the *Schoharie County
Historical Review* in the Fall-Winter issue of 1971.

Excerpts from the *Review:*

"The Pavilion Hotel, which has been erected with an eye single to the health and comfort of its patrons, fully realizing that in doing this its popularity and success is assured. It is constructed both of stone and wood, is three stories in height, and so arranged, both interior and exterior, that the most exacting person cannot take exception. The sleeping-rooms are all large and elegantly furnished. Many are arranged en suite, with private parlor, bath, etc.

"The house is lit throughout with gas, heated by steam when necessary, every room connected with the office by electric bell, hot and cold baths on every floor. . . .

"Sanitary Arrangements—This most important feature, as it should, has had special attention, both in and outside the hotel. . . .

"Entertainment—Fully realizing that our guests will require entertainments of various kinds, we have provided for them, among other things, a billiard room, bowling alley, and a large hall for charades, concerts, and dances. . . .

"Excursions will be arranged from time to time to Cooperstown (Otsego Lake), Sharon Springs, Richfield Springs, Saratoga, and other desirable places. . . .

"While under the head of 'entertainment,' we must not neglect to call your attention to the most interesting and wonderful feature in close proximity to the hotel, Howes Cave, a full description of which will be found further on. Here the student of nature can find rare studies.

"A nominal fee is charged to visit the cave, and guides are furnished at reasonable rates. Dressing rooms, with costumes, and other requisites, have been provided for visitors in the hotel, and immediately at the entrance to the cave."

It is interesting to speculate on the author's reason for including the following in his description of the guide services: *"No extortion is practiced or allowed in this particular."*

From the period 1890 until the turn of the century, the number of visitors to Howe's Cave gradually declined. As cement manufacture went on in high gear, a small community of management, quarry workers, and their families sprang up as the hamlet now known as Howes Cave.

The railway through the caverns' entrance no longer carried curious explorers. In a descriptive brochure from the period, the Howe's Cave Association noted: "This road is utilized for bringing out the remarkable deposit of clay that exists in a portion of the cave, [clay] which will be manufactured into building brick and Portland cement of a superior quality.

"From the quarries is taken some of the finest building stone in the state, and the stone from the mines is manufactured into the celebrated "Ramsey's hydraulic cement." These mines and quarries are interesting places to visit, and are inspected by many persons."

As a young man, Floyd Guernsey, from the Village of Schoharie, worked the quarries for the Ramsey organization. Many years later, in a July 15, 1935 letter to the new owners of Howe Caverns, Guernsey wrote:

"The location [of the Pavilion Hotel] was one of the finest places in Schoharie County, unspoiled by the hand of commercialism. Many times in my younger days, I visited the beautiful grounds above the entrance to the caverns, [where] the big hotel and extensive grove overlooked the beautiful and wide valley below.

"All this ... has been blasted away and entirely spoiled by the hands of commercialism in establishing a smoky and dirty cement plant. The cavern itself was entered for its valuables and turned to commercial uses."

Guernsey wrote of another, little-known attempt by the Ramseys to market the caverns' riches as building materials:

"Along the banks of the underground lake, there is a deposit of a fine grade of clay. On investigation by the Ramseys, they concluded that a fine grade of brick could be made out of this clay, so just outside the caverns they established a brick factory.

"A narrow track was laid in the cavern up to the clay bank of the lake, and a special rail car made ... for hauling out the clay. This business was active for about one year. These bricks proved to be worthless— the clay contained lime, which slacked and cracked the brick.

"Not a brick was sold.

"As a young man, I worked for the company making these bricks ... with another man. [I pushed] the little rail car up to the clay bank and loaded the clay. [Guernsey and his companion would then climb aboard and ride the gravity-pulled car back out to the cavern's entrance.]

"It has always been a deep regret to me that I had a hand in desecrating one of Nature's masterpieces."

The coming demise of Howe's Cave around the turn of the century is evident in the 1896 publication *Celebrated American Caves*, by the Reverend Horace Hovey. The book was a first in its field, and Hovey became regarded as the father of cave sciences. *Celebrated American Caves* contained the most accurate description of Howe's Cave at the time, as well as detailed reports on the other great touring caves of the period—Mammoth, Luray, Wyandot (Wyandotte), in Indiana, and others.

Hovey visited the cave with his son in 1880. His chapter on Howe's Cave contained many previously undocumented items and corrected several fallacies. While the report was complimentary overall, Hovey's truthful analysis generally dispelled the claim that Howe's size rivaled that of Kentucky's Mammoth Cave. From Hovey's *Celebrated American Caves*:

"A degree of disappointment must be confessed as to the entire dimensions of Howe's Cave. Some enthusiastic letter-writer once said that it was twelve miles long. The report on the geology of New York states that it has 'been explored to a distance of seven miles, and seems to extend further.' A clerical friend assured me that it was at least six miles long. It is recorded that one avenue 'never has been explored to its full extent, although a party once spent eighteen hours in it, traveling the whole time, and not reaching the end.' Finding that the proprietors themselves discredited these statements, and had no objections to my measuring the cave, I accordingly undertook the task, assisted by my son, with this result: that the total combined length of all avenues open to the public is only one mile and three quarters, and that there may be a mile or more of additional by-ways and tortuous crevices never shown to tourists; hence the owners are warranted in their honest advertisement that the entire length is about three miles."

Earlier in the same article, Hovey noted early "modern improvements" that had been undertaken by the Howes Cave Association, under Ramsey's ownership, including electric lighting:

"So much digging and blasting have been done between the entrance and the reservoir as to detract from the primitive wildness of the cave, and it too much resembles an unfinished railway tunnel. Gas, also, has been introduced, thus far with a pleasing effect ordinarily, though far less picturesque than torches and not free from danger. This appeared on the occasion of my first visit, which was in a company of a party of 400 excursionists, many of whom caught hold of the pipes overhead to steady themselves along difficult paths. This procedure disturbed the flow of gas. A number of jets were extinguished; and although frequently relighted, they could not be kept burning.

"The next day we examined critically the whole system of lighting up the cave in company with Dr. Lewis, the chemist of the Boston Gas Works, our conclusion being that it is safe enough, if the pipes and jets are not tampered with nor allowed to be eaten through by rust. We recommended the substitution of electric lights, which are now used."

In 1898, with cave tours and the resort business declining, the Howe's Cave Association reorganized as the Helderberg Cement Company. Tours through the cave were discontinued shortly thereafter, yet a continuous succession of owners quarried limestone from the hillside for cement, under several well-known quality brands. In 1900, fire again destroyed portions of the hotel, and tours through the cave were discouraged. The former Cave House hotel became a boardinghouse and was later converted into office space; in the early 1900s the quarry was the largest employer in Schoharie County.

No one knows exactly when, but sometime between 1910 and 1925, the first explosive charges in the limestone walls of the quarry face blasted into Howe's Cave. Over the years, approximately 300 feet of the "old" cave have been destroyed, including Washington's Hall, Cataract Hall, and the Music Room. Today, visitors see less than one-half of the original underground passage, and enter through a man-made entrance about one-mile north of the third Cave House Hotel, a portion of which still stands. Its windows have nearly all been broken, and crude boards have been hammered into place to discourage entry of trespassers. The floors are littered with the once-important papers of a former cement company, and the plaster walls are broken and peeling. A crude stairway— overgrown with vine, brush, and twisted limbs—leads not more than 30 feet down to the former entrance of old Howe's Cave. If one stands above the opening on a warm summer's evening, a refreshing current of the cool caverns' air can still be felt.

The original entrance is closed and gated. Through a man-made portal of limestone, less than 300 feet of "old" cave remains. Much of it has collapsed and is supported by decaying wooden timbers. The floor of the former North American Cement Co. quarry truncates the cave.

For many nineteenth-century visitors, these passages were once the introduction to the natural wonders of Howe's Cave. This section of the caverns was described in 1966 in *The Schoharie County Guide*, a publication complied by the Boston Grotto, a chapter of the National Speleological Society:

"Here and there may be seen bits of handrail and remnants of gas lights and gas tubing from the old commercialization. Beyond this giant hall, once known as the Lecture Room, there are many blocks of limestone rubble, the results of quarrying activities within the cave. High on the right-hand wall is a Gothic arch that leads to the "Wine Chamber" and to the "Bridal Chamber" where Lester Howe's daughters were married."

About 65 feet inside the entrance to old Howe's Cave is another cave entrance, to Barytes' Cave. Uncovered during mining operation in 1904, Barytes' Cave extends to the northwest approximately one-half mile, and was once mined for ore used in paint products. More on Barytes' Cave later.

Walking across the quarry leads to the back door of Howe Caverns, an artificial opening in the quarry wall where the "old" section of cave continues. The passage consists of about 1,800 feet of the original cave, left undeveloped, extending beyond the lake and the tourist route.

In the mid-1940s, cave explorer and author Clay Perry described his comical attempts to enter the commercial section of Howe Caverns through this man-made entrance:

"We tried it, one hot summer day, led by the intrepid Roger Johnson, who so charmed the guard who was there to keep foolish persons out, that he just didn't see us drive in to a point near the yawning entrance of the quarry and then walk in. We clambered up the rubble-strewn passage as far as we dared, mischievously intending to surprise Mr. Clymer and Mr. Hall (the caverns' managers) by sneaking in like boys under a circus tent.

"We had to retreat to the mine, stumbling over fossilized rocks, picking some up and pocketing them, thus plundering the cement company, which doubtless never missed them.

"In the mine the grinding machinery of the cement mill shook the very rock above our heads until we found ourselves looking cautiously up at the solid ceiling, again and again. Nothing fell. We came out after walking for perhaps a mile around the many pillars left to support the ceiling."

In the early 1900s, the wonders of world-famous Howe's Cave and the elegant accommodations of its Pavilion Hotel were no longer desired by curiosity seekers. Natural attractions—not only in upstate New York but throughout the country—declined in popularity among vacationing Americans, with more modern and urbane leisure activities taking their place. The large cities were reasserting themselves as home of the nation's cultural pursuits, and nature could be found—on display—in numerous museums.

Just after the turn of the century, an adventurous visitor would occasionally stop at the office of the Helderberg Cement Company to request permission to enter the once-famous cave. If a former tour guide could be located, permission might be granted, and a nominal fee was usually charged. Boys from the neighboring farms would play pirates and robbers inside the entrance, rarely venturing far beyond daylight.

The once-heralded discovery of Lester Howe had been ravaged by a series of owners, each more concerned with the forward movement of American industry than the protection of its resources. Smoke, soot, and cement dust rose from the kilns and boilers around the Howe's Cave quarry and covered the growing community of factory housing with a dirty gray ash.

Upstate New York's rival of Mammoth Cave was gradually being destroyed.

5

The Rebirth of Howe Caverns

THE TRAGIC STORY OF FLOYD COLLINS; THE MOSNER PLAN FOR REVITALIZING HOWE'S CAVE

Howe's Cave languished from the turn of the century to about 1920. It's beauty and profitability as a natural attraction had become secondary to the manufacture of cement.

Lester Howe died in 1888; his wife, Lucinda, died the following year at her daughter's home in Jefferson City, Missouri. Both were buried in the Cobleskill Cemetery. Ironically, according to Warren Howe, the claims against Lester's estate included a statement from the Howes Cave Association for $7.15. The statement is signed by association secretary and manager Charles H. Ramsey, the son of Joseph Ramsey, who had duped Howe of his property.

Elgiva, who wed railroad surveyor Hiram Dewey in the caverns' bridal chamber, had moved with her family to

Jefferson City shortly before her father died. They, too, were to make a regrettable business decision. Just before the move, Hiram was approached by young man from the neighborhood and asked to invest money in a speculative business venture. According to a family story retold by the couple's great grandson, Charles Dewey, the young man was going to "stop trains with air." Hiram was no fool, according to the family story, and he politely declined the young man's offer. The man was George Westinghouse, inventor of the air brake and founder of the multinational corporation that still bears his name. The Westinghouse home and laboratory was in nearby Central Bridge.

The other Howe daughter, Huldah, had also moved to Jefferson City with her family. Lester's son, Halsey, had married in 1865 and was living in Dunkirk, New York. Halsey died in 1913, his wife, Julia, in 1927. Both are buried at the Howe plot in the Cobleskill Cemetery.

Then, in 1925, a tragedy occurred that would eventually spur the rebirth of Howe's Cave. In the Mammoth Cave area of Kentucky, Floyd Collins set out to find a cavern worthy of commercial exploitation. While exploring alone a tight passage in Sand Cave, Collins became trapped. During the next sixteen days, the explorer's plight and rescue attempts captured national attention. Buried alive, Collins could see, hear, and converse with those leading rescue attempts. Most Americans suffered vicariously—through Collins—their own worst fears.

Sensationalist newspaper coverage fanned a national hysteria: hourly bulletins were eagerly awaited by millions listening to the new medium of radio; even Congress recessed to hear the latest word on the Collins situation. But the Collins debacle ended in tragedy: the explorer's lifeless body was pulled from Sand Cave on February 15. Floyd Collins immediately joined the ranks of America's folk heroes; his story, in many forms, has since been told many times and in many different media.

It was during the next several years that many of America's commercial caves were opened. Howe Caverns was one of them, pulled from decline and saved from continuing quarrying. The rebirth and successful commercial development of Howe Caverns during the years 1926–1929, can, in large part, be attributed to two remarkable individuals: John Mosner, of Syracuse, and Walter Sagendorf, of Saranac Lake.

It was Mosner who proposed the modern engineering developments that make the cave easily accessible—even comfortable—to the average visitor. Mosner was a steam-fitting and heating engineer, and the vice president and general manager of the Edward P. Bates Company, of Syracuse. Mosner's foresight is described in the *Story of Howe Caverns*, published in 1936 by the caverns corporation.

Then in his early twenties, Mosner toured Howe's Cave by torchlight in 1890 and was greatly impressed with its beauty. Mosner also toured the popular caves in Virginia and Kentucky before the turn of the century.

At about the time of the Collins tragedy, electric lighting was being introduced to many of the country's show caves. In 1927, Mosner again toured the commercial caves of the scenic Shenandoah Valley, which were now lit by electricity. Mosner's thoughts returned to Howe's Cave.

He remembered how difficult it had been to enter the cave through the nearly half-mile passage from the original entrance to the foot of the lake. Mosner predicted that Howe's Cave, with a shaft for elevators sunk at the inner end of the cave, and with electric lighting, would become a leading tourist attraction.

Mosner was an innovator, serious in dress and appearance, with a square jaw and large mustache. He talked about the cave incessantly, and plans were formulated and reformulated in his mind many times. He convinced others as well that his plan to revitalize Howe's Cave would work; the caverns' first officers included his boss, D. Cady Fulmer, and Virgil Clymer, a Syracuse attorney.

Walter H. Sagendorf provided the organization and business acumen for the Mosner plan. A successful Saranac Lake restaurateur, Sagendorf had lived in the Schoharie Valley area. His brother, John, owned the farm property on which the caverns' entrance lodge is now located. Both were familiar with the old Howe's Cave; as young boys they were among the many neighborhood cowboys, pirates, and robbers who had played inside the cavern's entranceway.

Sagendorf was the organizing force behind Howe Caverns, Incorporated, created to finance a $250,000 development with the sale of closed-stock shares. Sagendorf was elected first president of the corporation, and the Sagendorf name is still synonymous with Howe Caverns to this day. It has been a relationship of both family triumph and tragedy. John Sagendorf, secretary of the corporation, died in the caverns in 1930. The freak accident was linked to quarry operations at the caverns' original entrance, and is described later in this book.

Throughout 1926 and during the first half of 1927, Howes Cave was abuzz with talk of the caverns' reopening. Farm land was being purchased quietly, at prevailing prices, by persons unknown to the locals. By the time the first news story reached the publisher of the Cobleskill weekly newspaper, more than 1,500 acres to the north of the caverns' old entrance had been acquired. Most of the farm families who sold lands to the caverns' developers remained on their lands. Many of them, their descendants, and their relatives have been employed at the cave at one time or another. The names VanNatten, Nethaway, Crommie, Rickard, Lawyer, and Zeh are familiar to most residents of this rural community. In all, the caverns' developers paid $48,996 for the land rights to the property on the surface above the cave.

For many residents of the small community of Howes Cave, the cavern remained a source of considerable pride, despite its deterioration during the years 1900–1927. And throughout the county, a sense of local pride maintained the caverns' grandeur as being among the biggest and the best.

The first news to reach the public of the plans for the cave's reopening was announced with an eight-column banner headline on July 28, 1927, in the *Cobleskill Times*. The story generated tremendous excitement, and contained many of the rumors circulating the area, many of which later proved to be embarrassingly false.

According to the Cobleskill weekly newspaper, the developers' plans (which the *Times* estimated at over $1 million) called "for a new hotel, golf links, air-port, and a railway station to be located along the Delaware and Hudson tracks, two miles west of the Howes Cave station and village. The proposed site of the hotel and golf course commands an unusual view of the surrounding hills.... The new company is understood to have in mind a summer and winter business for visitors to the cave."

The article, headlined "Financial Group Plans to Reopen Howes Cave," reported the "elaborate plans" of a

Syracuse syndicate to "revive the one-time popularity of the cave, which is known to be the second largest in the world." Continuing the local conceit, the newspaper claimed that "compared with large natural caves in Virginia and even the Mammoth Cave in Kentucky, the immense cavern discovered by Howe is believed to possess greater wonders and furnishes a strong appeal to tourists."

Throughout the late summer months of 1927, Mosner, Clymer, Fulmer, and others from Syracuse met often with the Sagendorfs and other Howes Cave residents who had expressed a speculative interest in the reopening of the caverns.

The developers enlisted the services of Delevan C. Robinson, who was considered to be the local authority on the area's caves. Twenty years earlier, Robinson had conducted a survey of Howe's Cave on behalf of the state, which, according to the local newspaper, had considered making the caverns property a state park. Robinson led many of the trips through the cave, as developers sought to impress its wonders upon other potential investors. (Delevan "D.C." Robinson had a lifelong interest in caves. In the 1930s, he moved to Altamont, in Albany County, where he opened Knox Cave. With a roller-skating rink, and weekly square dances, Knox Cave operated successfully until the late 1950s.)

On October 11, 1927, Howe Caverns, Inc., was organized as a closed-stock corporation under charter of the laws of New York state. Officers were elected, directors were appointed, and a business office was established in Cobleskill. A speculative offering was published to raise $150,000 of the quarter-million dollars the corporation estimated it would take to make the caverns visit "about as easy, comfortable and clean as walking through the streets of a village."

On the corporation's prospectus, Robinson is listed as a
director and also as general manager, a post he never held.
Clymer became the caverns' first general manager, with
responsibility for its day-to-day operations. Walter Sagendorf
was elected president by the corporation's directors, and
Fulmer and Walter H. Cluett, of Dobbs Ferry, just north
of New York City, were elected vice presidents. Cluett's
family fortune had been made in the second half of the
nineteenth century in the shirt- and collar-making segment
of the garment industry. Cluett, Peabody, and Co., and its
sister firm, the Arrow Shirt Co., were headquartered in
Troy. Cluett had probably been brought into the corporation by Walter Sagendorf, whose Saranac Lake restaurant
and resort attracted many influential business people.

John Sagendorf was named corporation secretary, and
Clymer became the corporation's first treasurer. The first
board of directors consisted of the officers and Mosner, as
well as E. K. Hall, of New York City, and Richard Ward,
of Lawrence, Massachusetts. All are now deceased.

Corporate representatives began soliciting sales of stock
in the proposed Howe Caverns, offering 3,000 Class A and
3,000 Class B shares, both classes at $100 per share. (Class
A was the preferred share, guaranteed an $8 per year
dividend.) In 1927, $100 was a great deal of money;
investors were offered the subscription for $10—or 10
percent down—the balance in an equal percentage for the
next five months.

John Sagendorf's wife, Mabel, recalled: "It wasn't easy
to ask people to invest in the caverns—something which
most people had never seen—and having no way of knowing how successful it would be. There are very few people
living today who know all the work, worry and sleepless
nights that were involved."

Within weeks of incorporating, the new officers of Howe Caverns, Inc., were ready to publicly announce their plans for the cave. More than $60,000 had been raised by the developers, most of it solicited through the sale of shares in the Saranac Lake area, where Ausable Chasm was a popular natural attraction.

Walter Sagendorf and Clymer outlined plans to the business leaders of Cobleskill on the night of October 27 at a well-attended meeting of the Chamber of Commerce. The presentation, reported by the local newspaper, put to rest many of the rumors that had circulated about the development.

"Denying published reports concerning the erection of a hotel, golf links and other features near the entrance to the cave, Mr. Clymer stated that the company did not intend to go into these phases of the development at all," reads a portion of the *Cobleskill Times* article, "a pavilion for the sale of souvenirs and refreshments being the only building to be constructed."

The front-page story offers considerable insight into the business acumen Sagendorf and Clymer brought to the Howe Caverns corporation. Their presentation to the local business community, in which the two men covered all aspects of the development plans, must have been a long one.

A sampling from the *Cobleskill Times* article:

"In his talk to the local business men, Attorney Clymer went at length into the illumination phase of the cave's attractiveness, alluding to the Virginia caverns which are electrically lighted and produce gorgeous effects throughout the huge subterranean area. Colored lights and flood arrangements at proper locations, where the natural formations are most phe-nomenal, he said, made the Virginia caverns unusually attractive to tourists. Howe's cave, he declared, was favorably compared with the famous Luray Cavern in Virginia by several authorities, which were quoted from published volumes on the subject of caverns and magazine articles.

"Looking back into the old days before the advent of motor cars and provisions for electric lighting, the cave could not be compared [with the Virginia Caves], said Mr. Clymer."

Clymer told chamber members that the developers an-ticipated 200,000 visitors annually, and Clymer's estimate has proven remarkably true for nearly 60 years. After acquiring title to most of the caverns' property, Clymer continued, the corporation's officers surveyed the gate attendance at the three popular Virginia caverns—Luray, Shenandoah, and Endless.

"The visitors to the three principal caverns were counted as nearly as that could be done, and on one day the names on the register of one cavern was counted. These check-ups were made for one day in April and two days in August, about ten days apart, and the result showed approximately between four hundred and five hundred people had entered End-less Caverns in one day, about the same number in Shenandoah Caverns, one hundred of which had entered during the evening. The caverns are lighted by electricity and business is carried on evenings as well as day times.

"As the temperature in the caverns remains practically the same winter and summer, the business goes on 365 days of the year. At Luray Caverns the visitors were about as many as the other two caverns combined, there being about 300 automobiles at the entrance one day and over 800 visitors another day. We were informed that the visitors to the three caves mentioned totaled 370,000 last year.

"In order to get an idea of the probable number of visitors to Howe Caverns if they were open to the public, a check was made of the travel on the Lee Highway, which is the principal north and south highway nearest the three caverns mentioned, and also of the travel to the Cherry Valley and the Albany—Binghamton highways. The check showed that the two latter roads did fifteen times the traffic carried on the Lee Highway. We also find the density of population near Howe Caverns is much greater than near the Virginia caverns. Within a radius of three hundred miles of Howe Caverns there is a population of 26,000,000 people.

"*In other words, about one quarter of the population of the United States is within one day's automobile ride of Howe Caverns.*" [Italics added—Ed.]

Clymer and Sagendorf both stressed the value of the caverns' rebirth to the business interests of Cobleskill and the surrounding area. A $100,000 advertising and publicity campaign was planned, they said, to coincide with the cave's grand reopening.

Clymer closed the presentation.

"What I have stated will give you some idea of the tremendous financial advantage which will come to

Schoharie County because of the spending thousands of people will do in the villages through which they pass and in which they stop for a few hours or overnight. The farm, merchant, hotel, restaurant, garage, gasoline stations, and bank will be benefited, and each will be benefited to the extent that the traveling public is served on a fair basis and in a courteous manner. This no doubt is a trite saying, but it cannot be emphasized too often or too much. If the visitors find attractive stores and display windows, good restaurants and hotels, and he also finds courtesy and moderate prices at those and other places he trades, he will remember it and tell his friends, and the result and benefits will be continuous for Schoharie County.

"I would like to see the Chamber of Commerce, when the cave is reopened or before, start through the newspapers a "be courteous to the public" campaign. I suggest this not because the average individual is lacking in courtesy, but because we have got to do a little more than the average in order to make the traveling public speak of us in favorable terms, for otherwise one town is not different from another.

"And last, now that you have heard of this wonderful business which is to be located in Schoharie County, you should immediately begin to boost and keep on boosting for Howe Caverns and for your own locality."

6

Work Begins Underground

WORK BEGINS UNDER-
GROUND; ROGER MALLERY,
WORKER'S HERO; THE EN-
GINEERING STORY

Early in 1928, work in the caverns began in earnest.
The engineering firm of Smith, Golder, and Homburger, Inc., of Saranac Lake, began surveying the cavern;
Roger H. Mallery, of Howe Cave, was hired to "do
preliminary excavating necessary for construction of a new
entrance to the cavern." It was an exciting year in the
cavern's history.

Morris Karker was part of the caverns' work crew.
Karker later enjoyed the distinction of leading the first
group of tourists through the revitalized Howe Caverns in
1929. In 1979, a tour guides' reunion was organized to
coincide with the caverns' corporation's fiftieth anniversary
celebration. Karker, now deceased, wrote the following,
which was printed as part of a commemorative booklet.

HOWE CAVERNS AS I RECALL

"Sometime after 1925, rumors began to circulate in the community of Barnerville (where I then lived) that someone was interested in reopening the cavern as a commercial venture. Some farms and lands had been purchased in a quiet manner at a fair or prevailing price. But the first public knowledge that a determined effort was being made was when in the Fall of 1927, Palmer Slingerland, a resident of Bramanville and with a minor interest in the development, came into Charley Quackenbush's shop for the purpose of selling stock in the newly formed company. Charley was in accord with the venture, but for various reasons, did not think he could or should invest in it. I was there working with Charley and had no money at all, but knowing that soon our seasonal work would end, I suggested that I would willingly buy two shares of stock for $200, providing that if and when work started, I would be given employment so as to pay for them out of my earnings. Possibly, because the sale of stock was not moving very well and the company was anxious to enlist local support, my offer was accepted.

"A short time after January 1, 1928, I was advised to meet Mr. Homburger at the Howes Cave railroad depot and work under his direction. Mr. Homburger was a civil engineer and would survey the cavern. Homburger (Henry) and his crew of two brothers, John and Jim Kelly, did not appear on the designated train or day. I was directed to help Roger Mallery and his crew construct a pole shaft into the cavern ceiling, to regain access to the cavern; a cave-in had completely sealed off the only access to the cavern, so it was paramount this obstacle be overcome before anything else could be done. The cave-in occurred about 30 feet from the vertical east face of the quarry and about 400 feet from the former entrance. It was a hazardous task, but it was accomplished.

"I suppose Mallery and his crew were accorded appropriate recognition for this feat. During the winter and spring of 1928, Mallery and his crew completed the walks, laying walls, removing obstacles, to make all passageways reasonably safe and comfortable. My second day of work was meeting Homburger and his crew and all of us being led by Dellie (Delavan) Robinson for a preliminary exploration of a totally unfamiliar world. [Dellie, or D.C., Robinson had a lifelong interest in caves. In the 1930s he opened Knox Cave, near Altamont, to the public.] My apprehension climaxed during an incident which occurred when we reached the stone dam where the cement company had laid pipe for a water supply. There was a fairly deep pool in the stream bed below the dam; to get to the top, a 16-foot plank 12″ wide with cleats nailed on it (to prevent slipping) had been placed there. Dellie, a large man, over six feet, and weighing over 200 pounds, led the way. Midway up the plank, it broke and he fell completely submerged into the deep pool below. The rest of us were willing to run back but Dellie, dedicated to the task at hand, overcame his chagrin and discomfort, and after emptying his boots of water, completed the tour. We spent the remainder of the day at make-work jobs away from the silence and blackness of totally unfamiliar experience.

"The survey was a slow, time-consuming task. Angle stations had to be determined, then a hole drilled into the rock so as to insert brass rods securely and a prick point made to serve as exact point of angle. It was imperative that the survey be accurate, so that the test hole to locate the shaft for the new entrance be exact. The sightings between stations were numerous and often close, and it was difficult to see the line on the plumb-bob. Echoes made communication nearly impossible. Progress was slow. We were a month on the job, surveying just under one-mile of cavern passage.

"We then had to survey on the surface, to locate a drill hole for the elevator entrance. This did not take long. By applying simple mathematics, only a few shots were needed, along with accurate measurements to determine the exact position. Unfortunately, a math error was made, and the first test hole was drilled nearly 200 feet south of where it should have been. Much to the delay, embarrassment, and cost of those concerned, the error was corrected, and the next test hole came through the roof of the cavern exactly on target."

Editor's note: This report of the first test drilling conflicts with the surveyor's own report, which was published as part of the corporation's *Story of Howe Caverns*. Homburger's report appears later in this chapter.

Karker continued:

"There were a few weeks when Homburger had no

work for me, and I was assigned to the Mallery crew. I recall removing a six- or eight-foot pile of clay in front of the elevator stops, excavating the bridal chamber and the steps leading to it, and removing a 15-foot column of rock standing in the Winding Way. It was an unusual form of erosion, but unfortunately had to be removed to permit easier and faster traffic to the end of the Winding Way. It was hard, messy work, but not without interest and some fun. When Spring arrived, I helped Homburger survey for the highway leading up to the lodge. By then Byron Stickles, 'the carpenter boss,' who came from Syracuse appeared, and I went to work for him constructing the lodge. I worked under Stickles for better than a year, until it was nearly completed. John Sagendorf wanted me to train to work as a guide. I had some reservations concerning my aptitude and liking for the job, but agreed to try, as it would be an easy, clean, and reasonably secure job. . . .

"I acted as a guide for only a month. And when in 1932, I sold the shares I held, plus any interest or dividends that should have accrued, my association with Howe Caverns, Inc. ended. I cherish the memory of that long ago association, with so many men, now nearly all gone, engaged in a venture that has added much to the benefit of our meager rural economy, and wish for its continued success."

—Morris Karker, 1979

Working in the caverns under the most difficult of conditions was not without danger. The men were continually wet, muddy, and cold. They lost their balance and

THE HARP ON CRYSTAL LAKE—
This printer's woodcut, done about
1885, was used to illustrate the
chapter on Howe's Cave in the
first scientific treatise of caverns,
"Celebrated American Caves," by
Rev. Horace Hovey.
(Courtesy of Howe Caverns, Inc.)

Left, WALTER SAGENDORF—First
president of Howe Caverns, Inc.
A successful Saranac Lake resort
owner, Sagendorf was a native of
the Howes Cave area and had
played in the abandoned caverns
as a young boy. *Below,* plan and
section views of the caverns drawn
in 1906.
(Photo courtesy of Howe Caverns, Inc.)

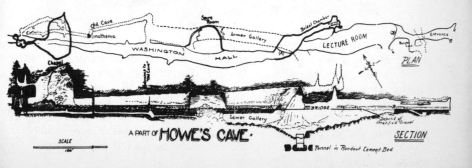

AT THE FOOT OF THE UNDERGROUND LAKE—from a series of photos taken in 1889 by famous Adirondacks photographer H. R. Stoddard.

Left, JOHN SAGENDORF, with an unidentified tourguide. Sagendorf was the owner of the farm property on which the modern caverns entrance and lodge is located. First secretary of the caverns' corporation, John and another employee were killed in the caverns in a freak accident shortly after the cave was reopened. The accident was linked to mining operations in the Howes Cave cement quarry. *Right*, ALTON "JIM" VANNATTEN—Nearly trapped in the cave by noxious fumes from the nearby cement quarry, VanNatten and another tour guide narrowly escaped the 1930 tragedy which claimed the lives of two men.

UNDERGROUND BOATING, 1930. The two-ton boats were assembled in the cave and named "Venus" and "Alcestis." Photo is from caverns' original post card series.

IN 1930, TELEPHONE LINES UNDERGROUND were considered such a modern engineering accomplishment that they merited a souvenir postcard. *Insert*, HENRY A. HOMBURGER —Surveyed the caverns in 1926 to determine the location for the new elevator entrance. He estimated the job would take 3 weeks; it took three months under unusual and difficult conditions.

(Photo courtesy Howe Caverns, Inc.)

fell in slippery mud. Boats capsized in the 42-degree lake. Bats flew about.

In a 1979 postscript to his original memoirs, Karker recalled catching Hank Homburger in a fall from the top of a 15- or 20-foot ladder he rigged over a chasm. "I kept his head and shoulders from striking [the] rocks below, but he hurt one knee badly and lost a big toenail in the fall."

As the underground drainage system for surface water from melting snow and heavy spring rains, the underground stream in the cave is subject to seasonal flooding. John Homburger, at the time just eighteen, assisted his older brother, Hank, in surveying. He recalled "brutal wet duckings" when rising floodwaters threatened to close the caverns entrance and trap workers inside. "Many a time . . . we led [the workers] out, each man grasping the belt or collar of the man in front and being pushed in turn by the nervous co-workers behind."

At about 2 P.M. on a warm, seasonably wet Monday, April 24, five of Mallery's employees unexpectedly appeared at the caverns' entrance, their work clothes entirely soaked in icy water. Frantic, the men sounded the alarm: sixteen workers were trapped at the farthest point from the entrance by a quickly rising current. Their exit blocked, the men sought refuge in one of the small construction shacks about a mile from the entrance. If the caverns' underground stream continued to rise—and outside weather conditions indicated it would—the stranded workers could be trapped for days, or worse, drown.

Gathering a rope, his lantern, and other supplies, Mallery entered the cave. The entrance passage, Washington's Hall, the Giant's Chapel, and Cataract Hall were easily traveled, the underground stream being siphoned off by numerous outlets deeper in the cave. Reaching Flood Hall,

Mallery could see the danger, and water was beginning to fill the passage. Just ahead lay the underground lake, and Mallery wondered if he had the strength to pilot the small boat moored there against the underground current.

By the time he reached the stranded crew of laborers, the shack in which they had sought refuge was almost completely cut off. In the passage between Mallery and his men, floodwaters came to within inches of the ceiling. Mallery tied the rope to the nearest anchor he could find and dived headfirst into the 42-degree current. Struggling upstream for about 20 feet, he finally reached the anxious workers. Together, they tied the other end of the rope, and one by one they were able to follow the line to safety. They emerged, cold and frightened, to a cheering crowd of their co-workers. Mallery was a hero, and news of his action reached newspapers around the state.

Most of the workers from out of town bunked in at Mrs. Louise Provost's boardinghouse, which operated for a few years in the former Cave House Hotel. "We had evenings to share our misery of bruised shins, wet clothes, holes torn in our boots, and the best ways of removing the taffy-like clay that stuck to our equipment, our bodies, and the walkways," the younger Homburger remembered.

Workers in the cavern came upon several unique finds. At the base of the elevator shaft, the initials of an early explorer with the date "1851" were discovered. Homburger, the caverns' surveyor, reported "one room at the end of a tortuous passage contained millions of bones of bats, covering the floor like pine needles in a forest." They had been preserved in layers of clay to the depth of several feet. An invitation to Harriet Elgiva Howe's wedding reception, September 27, 1854, was found in the clay in a section of the "old cave." This is now on display in the caverns' lodge, along with what is believed to be a photo of Harriet's wedding in the cave's Bridal Chamber.

On February 16, 1928, the *Cobleskill Times* reported on page one the discovery of a new rotunda in the cave. Although the "discovery" was obviously a news item placed by the caverns corporation, the article accurately described construction work in the cave at that time. Headlined "New Rotunda in Howe Cave," the *Times* story reported:

"Discovery of new chambers in Howe Cave during the period of reopening and reconditioning...has been announced by Howe Caverns, Inc. Although the 'rotunda' is well known to those who have visited the cave in years past, opening of further subterranean passages, especially of large size, is entirely new.

"With a force of fifty men at work, the repairing of walks and bridges in the world-famous Howe Cave is well under way to make visits by tourists during the coming summer not only safe but attractive. A well drilling machine is putting an eight-inch hole 100 feet through the ground at a point where the new entrance to the cavern will be constructed.

"Later, electric wires will lead into the cave through this opening and an illuminating system will be completed throughout the interior so that tourists will be permitted to view the wonderful natural formations by the use of colored and flood lights with attending grandeur such as produced in only a few other caves in the world, the nearest being located in Virginia.

CONTRACTOR BUSY

"After completing arrangements with Contractor

Roger Mallery, the Howe Caverns corporation is making rapid progress on the huge task of reconditioning and reopening the cave which has been closed to the public for many years. It is arranged that the work of excavating for the new entrance will proceed simultaneously with the electrical contract and reconditioning of paths and bridges, so that with the coming of late spring it is expected that the cavern will be nearly ready to receive visitors."

Additionally, the *Times* reported that caverns officials predicted the work would take only another four months (it took another year and four months). The corporation's tentative opening date, according to the newspaper, was July 1, 1928.

The article concluded: "A visit to the cave reveals the information that along with the rapid progress in getting the cavern reopened, comes considerable interest on the part of people residing in this part of the country as they are actually 'seeing the dirt fly.'"

In addition to the daring cave rescue of the workers caught by high water, contractor Mallery distinguished himself again during the caverns' commercial development. About three weeks after the rescue, the *Cobleskill Times* carried on page one the following social item:

"Recalling the days of Edward [sic] Howe, discoverer of the famous Howe Cave who arranged the marriage ceremony for his daughter in the Bridal Chamber, a similar event took place in the cavern last week.

"On Thursday evening in the same Bridal Chamber, Miss Margaret May Provost, daughter of Mrs.

Louise Provost of Howes Cave and Roger Mallery, son of Mr. and Mrs. Clarence S. Mallery of Binghamton, were united in marriage by the Rev. F. M. Hagadorn of Cobleskill.

"Those witnessing the ceremony were the bride's mother, Mrs. Louise Provost, her brother, Francis Provost; and John J. Sagendorf, one of the directors of Howes Caverns, Inc.

"Mr. Mallery is the contractor in charge of the work of cleaning up the cave. Mrs. Mallery was graduated from Cobleskill high school in the class of 1922 and from New York State college for Teachers class of 1927.

"Following a honeymoon in New York City and other points of interest they will reside in Howes Cave."

There was a lighter side to working in the cave as well. Newcomers were taunted by their co-workers with wild tales of bottomless pits and of monsters and blind fish that attacked workers from the lake. Snakes, frogs, and worms found their way into lunch boxes. Backpacks often carried an additional brick or two. Rumors were circulated that payday would be pushed back by a week, or that workers would be paid in stock certificates that would be honored at the end of fifty years.

Few visiting the caverns today can fully appreciate the magnitude of the commercialization of Howe Caverns. Many fail even to consider that it took place during a period of American history in which, in many homes, electricity and telephone service were luxuries.

During the past sixty years, minor changes have continued to be made to the original cave: the introduction of elevators, paths, hand rails, and electric lighting. Bricks— 88,000 of them—replaced gravel paths when, in 1938, the cave flooded to the ceiling and washed the gravel out the natural entrance. In 1972, a man-made tunnel connected the end of the Winding Way with the elevators to ease traffic through the cave. And twenty-four miles of the 1928 wiring system was replaced and updated in 1975.

The "Engineering Story," portions of which follow, was first published in the Howe corporation's *Story of Howe Caverns*, copyright 1936. It was written by H. A. Homburger.

ENGINEERING STORY

"The problem confronting the Caverns developers was that they owned several miles of natural caverns located somewhere underground about a half mile from the then only entrance, but no one knew in what direction or under what property the cave extended. The original entrance passageway presented so many difficulties that only a few persons were interested in exploring it. How could these beautiful caverns be reached by large numbers of people?

"The only way was to follow Mr. Mosner's plan, sink a shaft and install elevators at the extreme inner end of the caverns. The place where such a shaft should be built could be located only by surveying the caverns and using the data to definitely fix the spot on the surface. At that point a well hole, called a bore hole, would have to be drilled in order to check the accuracy of the survey, and to determine the character of the ground through which the shaft would be sunk.

"The first trip is as fresh in my mind today as the day I took it, and it will always remain one of the outstanding experiences of my life. After a preliminary trip to determine the lay of the land and the conditions, work was begun about January, 1928. I had expected to complete the surveying in two, possibly three weeks, little realizing that we should spend three months in what was probably the strangest conditions we shall ever experience.

"With my two assistants and some equipment, including flashlights, I again made my way to the Caverns by the original opening. Certainly that trip was a revelation to us. The entire day was spent in laying out and marking the approximate location of traverse stations for the survey, and in becoming acquainted with some of the difficulties provided by Dame Nature in a domain over which she alone had presided for untold thousands of years.

"During the day I was compelled to change my impressions of the magnitude of the job. Some parts of the Cavern seemed impossible to survey. There were canyons and gorges: huge piles of rock and debris to get around; a thousand foot lake to cross with little or no shore line; raging torrents of water through places with scarcely room to crawl or squeeze; mud, the stickiest and slipperiest I had ever encountered; and over all a Stygian darkness which absolutely killed light. To make it more pleasant thousands of bats flying frantically around, now in darkness, now in a beam of light, the flittings and chirpings giving one an impression of a tomb disturbed, and with vengeful spirits working near.

"A very much impressed, tired, wet, and mud

covered trio of surveyors emerged that night to the welcome sunset of a beautiful winter day.

"The main location traverse to locate the bore hole [on the surface] consisted of fifty-two stations, [measuring only about 4,100 feet of cave]; some several hundred feet long, and others only ten or fifteen feet long.

". . . On account of the roar of the water, at times terrific, coupled with the confines of the caverns, it was impossible to communicate directly by voice for any distance and my experienced assistants were certainly a big help because of their understanding of signals and the results required. They showed a very keen interest, sometimes amounting to genius, in overcoming the obstacles. It is certainly a trying situation, after an hour's work making a setup, slung by rope to operate, to find an assistant doing something wrong, not knowing it and no way to communicate with him. Truly in such a situation, patience is a virtue.

"Due to the nature of the surrounding surface country, with its seams and sinkholes, the brook through the caverns formed the drainage medium for several square miles of countryside. Frequently we would enter in the morning after a freezing night and scarcely dampen our boots, and then, unknown to us the outside temperature would moderate, setting loose thousands of rivulets . . . so that some days at 3 o'clock we could not return without swimming or wading to our shoulders in nice, icy water, and a darkness blacker than black.

"This condition at first bothered us somewhat, but we discovered that by waiting until five o'clock or later, when there was freezing temperature outside, that the water would subside enough to let us pass comfortably in our hip boots. . . .

"On one occasion, it took three days of lying and crawling on our stomachs, using a specially-made tripod about ten inches high, to survey a single station. We could scarcely breathe for fear of making an impenetrable fog through which we could not see for five feet. Some passages led to rooms so high that our strongest spotlights could not penetrate the gloom of their roofs. The floor of some rooms was so thick with clinging, sticky clay that it would pull off our boots, and to walk at all meant to hold them on with the hands.

"During the period of our surveying, the building of the caverns walks was commenced by two shifts of workmen. By this time temporary electric lights had been installed and work on the final lighting scheme was well started. . . .

"Our traverse closing line was about four thousand feet in length, and after three weeks drilling with a six inch well drill at the surface point we had designated, we had the satisfaction of seeing the bore hole punched through the caverns roof within three inches of the spot we had marked. It was to me one of the most satisfying sights I ever had, as it was the culmination of six weeks of extremely trying work and it was evidence that our labors had been carefully and correctly carried on. A careful record of the drill's progress through the ground was kept daily for ground study and proved most useful information. . . .

"Practically all of the wire and cable [for the caverns lighting system], many miles of it, were passed down through the bore hole and rewound on a reel on the floor of the caverns. All the cement and most of the gravel used in making the railing ties were poured down the same hole. A telephone line, the only means of communication with the surface, was later threaded through the opening and proved to be of inestimable value. Later when the bore hole was no longer needed to pass material through the caverns, and the elevator shaft was under construction, water lines were put through the bore hole....

"The hole is capped today on the surface near the caverns lodge, and is a reminder to those who know of the hard work and perseverence necessary to locate that particular point; to us who remember the days of darkness and wet; of the hours of crushing silence; of boats capsizing in the lake; of the wading in the swollen torrents; of the bats flying about and striking our body or face; of the discomforts sustained; but above all the friendships made to last a lifetime."

Digging the elevator shaft posed additional problems. Karker remembered: "The shaft was dug about 20 feet south of the bore hole. There, an unfortunate rock ledge [was encountered and] dropped off... so that instead of finding bedrock close to the surface, as the bore hole indicated, it was not found until 60 to 70 feet down." According to Karker, thousands of feet of "strong and costly timbers" were used to crib the sides of the shaft, and keep clay and mud from falling in on the workers.

The 156-foot elevator shaft, its steel and concrete housing and stairwell (with platforms for emergency stops along the way), were built at a cost of $160,000, or about $1,100 per foot. Thirty-four hundred tons of cement and

105 tons of steel were used to construct the entrance shaft, which would replace the caverns' original, natural entrance.

With the completion of the elevator shaft, work progressed more rapidly; makeshift electrical lighting was installed, and a telephone line was strung to let workers talk to those on the surface. Although installation of the two elevators for carrying paying visitors was many months away, a gas-powered winch and hoist carried work crews to and from the surface in a huge bucket. The bucket-ride took laborers directly into the main portion of the cave, as we see it today, and saved workers a tremendous amount of time. The shaft eliminated the long, wet, and muddy trip from the old entrance to Howe's Cave.

The installation of the elevators marked a major milestone for the developers, and the accomplishment highlighted nearly a year of rugged labor under the most difficult of conditions. The elevator entrance was the engineering cornerstone of Mosner's plan to revitalize the cave, and its completion signaled for developers the nearing realization of a dream.

7

The Grand Opening

**THE GRAND OPENING; TRIUMPH
AND TRAGEDY**

C ontrary to the optimistic reports in the local newspapers, Howe Caverns didn't open that July 1 in 1928.
As a result, the fall and winter of that year and the spring
of 1929 were busy months for the work crews and staff of
Howe Caverns, Inc.

The public's interest in the cave was continually aroused
through a series of promotional spots on the new medium
of radio, specifically on *The National Home Hour*, broadcast
in New York's Capital District on WGY. Businesses along
the "Susquehanna Trail," the Binghamton-to-Albany highway, were urged by the newspapers to plan and promote
for the coming tourist boom. They responded with a
vengeance. A local pharmacist advertised: "We prescribe a
visit to Howe Caverns." A Bradner's hardware store advertised: "The Sun Never Shines in Howe Caverns. . . . But
for comfort and appearance, protect your home or business place with awnings."

Arthur Van Voris, a Cobleskill hardware store owner and local historian, assembled a team of explorers for a newspaper series on the "lesser caverns of Schoharie County." In his mid-twenties, Van Voris was small in stature, with a triangular-shaped head, that began as a narrow, rounded jaw and chin; a neatly trimmed mustache topped off a small mouth, and his head was covered handsomely with thick, curly, auburn hair. He wore wire-rimmed glasses in the fashion of the day.

Accompanying Van Voris were Edward A. Rew—an employee of the Cobleskill Post Office—and the three "VanNatten Boys," who owned farm property in the cave country near the Howe Caverns estate. An account of their exploits appeared about once every other week in the Cobleskill newspaper. A promotionally enhanced compilation of the series was also published by the Bright Star Flashlight Company, of Hoboken, New Jersey. The twelve-page brochure, *Cave Exploring with Bright Star Flashlights*, invited readers to enjoy "the interesting story of these intrepid explorers of the almost unknown caverns in Schoharie County, New York."

Bright Star had an interesting innovation: a belt-and-harness attachment that left "Both Hands Free," according to their advertising materials. The brochure highlights "A Few of the Thousands of Uses of Bright Star Flashlights." A portion of the copy reads, "Both hands free! When the belt is slipped through both loop and ring hangers, light is cast on ground ahead and both hands are free."

Van Voris and his fellow explorers filed reports on four "lesser caves": Selleck's, Ball's, Benson's, and Nameless Caverns. In each, Bright Star Flashlights and batteries performed with "eminent perfection . . . always disclosing some new and entrancing detail at each turn of the light."

Van Voris was most impressed with Nameless Caverns, the entrance of which lies only about a mile to the northeast of the Howe Caverns' entrance lodge. "The glory and grandeur of this cavern!" he wrote. "Continuing for the entire half to three quarters of a mile to the far end, none of us had ever thought to behold such a gorgeous abundance of stalactites and stalagmites—countless hundreds of them!

"Words are all too inadequate," he concluded, "to describe what we saw in Nameless Cavern." The article on Nameless Caverns ran as the last of the newspaper series. Van Voris followed it up with an article the following week on Lester Howe's fabled Garden of Eden cave.

Meanwhile, at the Howe Caverns estate, the contractors were putting the final touches on the combined entrance lodge, gift shop, and coffee shop. A. J. Brockway, of Syracuse, was the architect. Before the opening, a promotional brochure described:

"The Entrance Building, being erected on the hill which forms the miles of roof of the Caverns, commands a 20-mile view of the valley below and the mountains beyond.

"The style selected by the architect was inspired by the wonderful old manor houses of England, combining a use of materials to give not only attractiveness, picturesqueness and dignity, but also suggest the welcome so characteristic of Old England. In order that hospitality will be the outstanding impression there is provided a large spacious lounge for the arriving visitors, with high, timbered ceiling such as is found in the Great Halls of the English houses. A huge stone fireplace at one end completes the picture of contentment and warm friendliness that will greet all visitors.

"The tea room, as well as the lounge, opens directly upon a broad, flower-bordered terrace which extends an hundred feet across the south front of the building.... During the winter months, probably many winter sports will be arranged for."

A private roadway from the highway to the caverns' estate was being constructed. It was an exciting time, as final preparations were under way for a grand opening, rescheduled for Memorial Day, May 27.

Throughout these busy months, Roger Mallery, the general contractor, workman's hero, corporation stockholder, and bridegroom in the caverns' first wedding since 1854, was noticeably absent.

Brochures, maps, and other promotional literature were prepared. In the days before color photography, color inks were added on the printers' press to black and white photographs, creating "natural color" postcards. General Manager Virgil Clymer appears in the earliest of the postcard series.

Chauncey Rickard, of Middleburgh, was hired to write the tour guides' spiel, and he prepared the first staff of caverns' guides for the day of the grand opening. He was a big, imposing man, with thick, black eyebrows that darkened his deepset eyes. Rickard was born on a poor backroads farm and had only a fifth-grade education. He was largely self-educated and nurtured his talents in the theater and the fine arts. He wrote flowery essays on local history, and composed and directed many community plays and pageants.

Chauncey was a student of mythology, and much of the caverns' original presentation included obscure references to the Gods of ancient Greece. Many of the paying customers in the modern caverns' early years probably found an embarrassing inconsistency between Rickard's jaunty prose and his imposing physical stature. His tour-guide presentation included such loquacious tidbits as the following recitation from the boat ride:

"We now enter the Hall of Adonis, a choice portion of the lagoon, for here Venus has been lavish with her beauty. It is the hall of the beloved youth, Adonis, who when killed in the chase, the goddess sprinkled nectar into his blood from which flowers sprang up. The ceiling of the abode of Adonis is encrusted with formations typifying the flowers which sprang from the beautiful votive."

There were six guides originally, hand-picked by the caverns' management. Rickard was head guide; Morris Karker was next in line, and the others were Will Kilmer, Omer Youmans, Alton (Jim) VanNatten, and Dave Kniskern. Rickard had the unenviable task of training five young recruits, fresh from the farm, to make the eloquent pitch on behalf of their new employer. It was probably no easy job; and Chauncey was insistent that the guides' presentation be *exactly* as he had written it. A former caverns' manager recalled the young guides rehearsing their lectures to the trees in the woods by the cave, at Rickard's direction.

"With his [Rickard's] sense of dramatics, he could really put it over. Many people were impressed, and said so. It was not so with the rest of us. Lacking Chauncey's talent...it was an embarrassment to see the look of disgust on visitor's faces," Morris Karker recalled.

The cave guides received $1.92 per day, plus tips, or nearly twice the prevailing wage for farm hands at the time. Guides had to pay $27 for their own military-like uniforms, or they could rent them for ten cents per day from the caverns corporation. Many of the first guides boarded at the VanNatten farm, just across the valley from the lodge.

Finally, the much-awaited grand reopening of Howe's Cave was set, May 27, 1929. It marked the culmination of more than two years of organization, planning, and hard labor, and an expenditure of nearly one-quarter of a million dollars.

Karker, who was there, remembers the excitement, the eager crowds, and an ironic twist of fate that occurred on the morning of the big day:

> "Chauncey met his party of officials and notables, gave his welcoming talk, entered the elevator, and went down into the cavern. I followed with the second party. But a lady in Chauncey's party was taken sick while descending in the elevator, and while he was returning with his party, my group, the second party, was the first to make the trip through the cavern.
>
> "If there is any honor to be gained by the distinction, it belongs to Chauncey, and I would not detract from his record by a simple quirk of fate."

The corporation's grand opening on that day was a tremendous success. More than two thousand visitors toured the cave that was made famous by Lester Howe nearly a century earlier.

With their work completed, the numerous engineers, contractors, workmen, and corporation staff were justifiably proud. Mother Nature's challenge had been accepted and overcome; her handiwork had been cleaned, scrubbed, and made "more beautiful" by modern presentation; the beauty of Howe's Cave could now be seen by well-dressed men and women in "comfortable shoes," according to the promotional literature.

The cavern's modernization became almost as strong a sales point as the beauty of its formations. In a postscript to the chapter "Engineering Story" from the corporation's *Story of Howe Caverns*, the editor notes: "This thrilling and fascinating story will impress the reader with the magnitude of perils braved, and obstacles overcome to make the caverns trip pleasant, comfortable, and safe."

Postcards, brochures, and booklets boasted of underground telephone lines. An entire chapter of the *Story of Howe Caverns* is dedicated to the power and voltage requirements of the cave's lighting system. The chapter also notes, "Two Otis gearless traction elevators which are provided with three speeds, convey visitors to and from the Caverns level. If desired the elevators can be dropped the length of the shaft in 30 seconds and returned in the same time."

A promotional map, *All Roads Lead to Howe Caverns*, printed two decades later, noted many of the particulars:

"A private roadway costing $20,000.

"Howe Caverns Lodge, costing $60,000, equipped like a modern country club for your convenience and comfort.

"A huge concrete elevator shaft extending 156 feet into the earth, containing two powerful electric Otis elevators and 245 steel and concrete steps, costing $160,000.

"An auxiliary electric plant exclusively for Howe Caverns. More than 1,500 electric lamps provide illumination, many of them 500 candle-power, 24 miles of cable and wire (much of it enclosed in lead to protect it), 35 transformers of 220 K-W capacity, and 101 switches. The wiring and switches are installed on the block system, enabling the guides to emphasize interest spots and places.

"Brick walks throughout; steel and concrete bridges. The walks are mainly built beside and above the bed of the underground stream. Along the walks are iron railings, set in concrete ties buried in the walks to insure ridigity. The walks, bridges and railings cost $80,000.

"On the Lake are two modern flat-bottom boats, each accommodating 18 passengers and 2 boatmen, who propel the boats with poles like the gondoliers of Venice. The boats were constructed in sections and assembled at the head of the Lake.

"Telephones, located at frequent convenient places throughout the Caverns, connect with the Lodge.

"On busy days from 70 to 80 people are employed to look after the comfort of visitors, including a staff of experienced, courteous and uniformed guides. Six men are required to handle the parking of cars."

Original postcards from the decade of the 1930s also proudly picture a unique byproduct of the modernization of Howe's Cave: underground plant life, which grows as a result of the heat generated from the lighting system. Today, the plant life is overabundant; the maintenance crew regularly pours a mild acid on the lichens, moss, and ferns that have spread throughout the cave.

John Mosner's vision of modernization and Walter Sagendorf's business plan for Howe's Cave were proved successful. Again, the cave was to become a profitable commercial enterprise. Upon the grand reopening of Howe's Cave, the Howe Caverns Corporation immediately established itself as the proprietor of a leading tourist attraction. More than 77,000 people toured the cave during its first year of business under corporate ownership. Today, nearly a quarter of a million people continue to tour the cave each year.

At 5 A.M. on a very cold Thursday, April 24, 1930, workers at the North American Cement Company, in the hamlet of Howes Cave, exploded a seven-and-a-half-ton compound of quarry gelatin, manufactured by DuPont. The charge toppled 160,000 tons of limestone from the hillside of the quarry that surrounds the abandoned caverns' property and former entrance.

As remote as the possibilities of a rockfall were, officials at the North American plant had met recently with Howe Caverns general manager Virgil Clymer. The cement company agreed that blasting would take place in the early morning hours, and not during the course of the daily tour schedule at the cave.

On that same morning, more than a mile to the northwest, the caverns' electrician, Owen Wallace, thirty-five, entered the cave shortly after 8 A.M. to conduct his daily inspection of the lighting system, to replace burned-out lamps, and to prepare for the coming business day. As he left the elevators, Wallace punched the magnetic switch to light the Vestibule, and walked alone down the short flight of steps into the main cave passage. Being alone in a cave, even a well-lit one, can produce an unnerving feeling. One hundred and sixty feet below the surface, the only sound is the gurgle of an underground stream. The imagination can play strange tricks.

Turning on the lights ahead of him as he walked, Wallace quickly passed the Balancing Rock, the Hands of Tobacco, and the Sentinels at the end of a deep chasm. Nothing seemed unusual. Standing at the base of the Rocky Mountains, he hit the switch to light Titan's Temple, the caverns' largest chamber, which stood before him by about 200 feet. He coughed, cleared his throat, and continued ahead, to the southeast. Wallace walked down a flight of stairs and into the Gallery of Titan's Temple. He admired two stalagmites—the Chinese Pagoda and the Leaning Tower of Pisa, then watched the passage ahead of him light up as he pushed the switch. Again, he coughed. This time his throat burned slightly, and he felt tired and dizzy. Wallace coughed again, and his breathing became difficult. His lungs were racked. He gasped desperately for breath. Retreating, he climbed down over the railing, hoping to reach the caverns water for its life-saving oxygen.

Seeping its way underground through the intricate maze of the caverns' passages and fissures was a deadly combination of carbon monoxide and nitrous oxide gases: a strange, unforeseen, chemical reaction resulting from the cement company's early morning detonation and the unseasonably cold weather, which was drawing the colder air into the 52-degree cave.

Corporation Secretary John Sagendorf, forty-two, entered the cave shortly after nine that morning, also alone. After all, nothing was suspect; he was probably curious about the progress Wallace was making. Perhaps the electrician had discovered problems with the caverns' lighting system. He walked quickly through the first quarter mile of cave.

Around 9:30, still no word had been heard from either

men, and tour guide Alton "Jim" VanNatten, twenty-five, entered the cave.

VanNatten returned to the surface at 9:45, choking and gasping, barely able to speak. He had found Sagendorf, lying face-down and unconscious near a flowstone formation known as the Bell of Moscow. Immediately, two other employees, Adam Kennedy and William Wambo, made the descent, hoping to pull the two victims to the surface. The pair returned within minutes, also suffering the effects of the noxious gases that had entered the cave. The three were rushed to an Albany Hospital for treatment; they later recovered.

Meanwhile, Clymer placed emergency calls to the local fire department and rescue squads, and to better-equipped squads from the nearby cities of Schenectady and Albany. Gas masks for the rescue efforts were flown in from Schenectady by Victor Rickard, manager of the Schenectady Airport.

News of the accident spread rapidly throughout the area, and the newspaper offices of the *Cobleskill Times* were besieged with requests for information. The highway leading to the caverns' entrance was soon filled with cars, the *Times* reported, "many of them newspapermen from nearby cities seeking information." After all, just four years earlier, William "Skeets" Miller, the reporter who had covered the tragedy of Floyd Collins at Sand Cave, Kentucky, had received a Pulitzer Prize for Journalism.

At 11:30, when Captain William Arndt of the Schenectady fire department arrived on the scene with four of his men, Wallace had been in the cave over three and one-half hours. With masks and oxygen tanks, Arndt and his men were the first squad adequately equipped to undertake the hazardous rescue attempt. Shortly after noon, Sagendorf was pulled from the cave; minutes later Wallace was returned to the surface.

By then, in addition to the caverns' staff, relatives, and scores of the curious, a twenty-man rescue crew had assembled at the caverns' lodge, including some medical personnel. A rescue squad from the North American Cement plant had arrived to offer their assistance. Rickard, the pilot, returned to Schenectady by plane for additional medical supplies, as efforts to resuscitate Sagendorf began.

One newspaper reported: "Volunteers worked unceasingly with inhalators, oxygen tanks, and applied the prone pressure method of resuscitation." Efforts continued, frantically, through the early evening. Finally, at 7:45 P.M., nearly twelve hours after Owen Wallace entered the cave, Dr. H. Judson Lipes, of Albany, pronounced both men dead at the scene.

The following week John Sagendorf, husband, and father of four young boys, was buried on his farm property overlooking the Howe Caverns estate. The memorial service was well attended and given prominent, front-page coverage by the Cobleskill newspaper under the headline "Sagendorf Funeral Services Largely Attended at Residence Near Caverns He Held Dear." Fitting remarks were offered by the Reverend F. M. Hagadorn, who noted that Sagendorf, as a caverns guide, had helped others marvel at the works of God. Upon his death, the Reverend Hagadorn pontificated, "A Supreme being had become the Guide, leading to higher and greater wonders of God in the Life beyond."

The tragedy was filled with sad ironies. Dr. Lipes was a brother-in-law of Sagendorf's. Sagendorf and Wallace were cousins. Both lifelong residents of the area, they had played together in the undeveloped cavern as young boys.

Newspaper accounts listed "Death by Unknown Causes" as the official verdict of the tragedy. A report from Albany noted:

"What gas killed the two men may never be known.

"Officials of the [cement] company insist that there are no fumes from dynamite which would make men helpless so suddenly that they could not reach safety.

"The men... showed signs of carbon monoxide poisoning, indicating a gas given off by something having been burned. There was also another gas present, some nitrous oxide, it is believed. No natural gases have ever been found in the caverns.

"R. A. Bloomsburg, New York Power and Light Company safety superintendent who directed the futile resuscitation work, regards the presence of noxious gases in doubt. 'From appearances, it would seem as if carbon monoxide was present,' explained Mr. Bloomsburg, 'and there may have been some nitrous oxides, which in combination, might have produced another gas. Ordinarily the explosion of dynamite does not give off poisonous gasses, but the situation in the cave was unusual. It was a cold day, cold air would be drawn into the crevasses and the warm air in the cavern rises. I think the possibility of any gas pocket in the cavern is remote.'"

The caverns' air was tested the following day and declared safe. Good crowds on Memorial Day weekend of the following month, according to one newspaper, indicated that the caverns' business had not suffered as a result of the tragedy. The chances of the chemical and atmospheric conditions that produced the deadly gases occurring were one in a million. But the caverns' management would take no chances. A large (approximately 12-foot-by-12-foot) ventilating fan was installed beyond the commercial section of the cave. With a reversible motor, the fan forces air both from the cave and through it. On hot days, the fan blows cool caverns air into the lodge and gift shop, reminisicent of Lester Howe's early efforts to air-condition the Cave House Hotel.

Mabel Sagendorf, John's widow, never remarried. Working at the caverns' gift ship until well past retirement age, she raised four sons on the family farm on Sagendorf Corners' Road. At this writing, Mabel, still going strong at ninety, is the only surviving member of the families of the caverns' original developers. All of the Sagendorf boys worked at the cave before going on to other careers.

Jim VanNatten, the tour guide who managed to return to the surface to sound the alarm, worked for the caverns corporation for many years. Even after his retirement as manager of the Howe Caverns motel, and until the mid-1970s, VanNatten would return to the cave each Memorial Day to conduct the first tour. After several years in a Cobleskill nursing home, VanNatten died in March, 1990.

The caverns' Bell of Moscow was renamed. Since the tragedy, it has been known as the "Giant Beehive."

Production continued at the cement quarry, through a succession of owners, and production peaked at two million barrels per year in the 1950s. While there has never been any danger to the caverns, the author can remember during the early 1970s sitting at night, in the picnic area of the caverns' estate, waiting for the sound of the quarry siren. The shrill whistle was to announce the impending blast; over a mile away, the explosive charge was barely audible. Then, a minute's wait. The ground would rumble and heave slightly before again settling, all within the space of just a few seconds.

Over the years, the cement produced of Howe's Cave limestone has received numerous awards for its quality. But in 1976 the quarry was no longer profitable, and the Penn-Dixie Cement Company closed it, throwing about 140 employees out of work. A new owner, Flintkote, continued to run the kiln and processing plant but ceased mining operations. In 1986, Flintkote closed the doors of the plant, and the 120-year-old cement industry in the Village of Howes Cave was ended.

Today the quarry stands unused, leaving a gaping hole in the countryside hundreds of acres wide, and about a half-mile deep. Fires no longer burn in the kilns; steam, gas, and cement dust no longer fume from the smokestacks and exhaust towers. The engines and turbines that smashed limestone to powder no longer grind. And the dilapidated cement quarry offices in the former Cave House Hotel are no longer occupied by busy managers, secretaries, and clerks.

8

The Early Years

COMPETITION AND CAVE WARS OVER THE TOURIST DOLLAR

S uccess breeds imitation. The reopening of Howe Caverns quickly prompted the development of three other commercial caves in the immediate vicinity. Two have since failed; a third, Secret Caverns, remains an active and aggressive rival for the tourist dollar.

Just months before the grand reopening of Howe's Cave, contractor Roger Mallery left the corporation's employ. According to Morris Karker, Mallery had expected to be awarded the $125,000 contract for excavation and construction of the elevator shafts. "But management deemed he lacked adequate equipment or experience to handle the job, or possibly other reasons, and awarded the job to a Pennsylvania company whose business was constructing mine shafts," Karker wrote.

Mallery, then thirty-three, would open his own cave, he decided. With landowner Leon Lawton, he developed another Schoharie County cavern during the winter of 1928 and early spring of 1929.

Only about two months after the grand reopening at Howe, the *Cobleskill Times* carried this article:

NEW CAVERN
OPEN TO PUBLIC
SECRET CAVERNS NEAR HOWE
CAVE HAS MANY
ATTRACTIONS

"Another cavern has been opened to the public in Schoharie County and promises to become one of the important natural wonders in the state. The name has been designated as Secret Caverns, and is located one mile north of the Howe Cave village, near Cobleskill.

"The cavern was first opened to the public last Sunday after being in preparation since last winter by Roger H. Mallery and Leon Lawton upon whose farm the cave is situated. It is stated that one hundred visitors viewed the cavern on the opening day.

LOCATION KEPT SECRET

"It seems that years ago Lester Howe, the discoverer of the famous Howe Cavern was accustomed to remark that he knew of a nearby cavern, but insisted on keeping its location a secret, and from this information comes the name of the present cavern, as it is believed that this is the subterranean wonder which Howe had in mind at that time.

"Mr. Mallery being a contractor, accustomed to

building bridges and various construction work, has devoted his time and energy to the opening of the cavern for the past several months. By the use of compressed air drills and a certain amount of blasting, the passageways through the cavern have been enlarged, so that one may pass through in comfort and with perfect safety, there being but a few places where it is necessary to stoop down.

"The natural formations in Secret Caverns are very unusual and many of them resemble objects such as animals and buildings together with an endless number of stalactites and stalagmites in various shapes and patterns. One unusual feature of Secret Cavern is two large grottos which extend upward a distance of over 50 feet.

"Opening Secret Cavern will doubtless appeal to additional thousands of visitors to come to Schoharie County and visit this newly opened natural wonder."

Despite the implications of Mallery's claims, Secret Caverns is not a "bigger and better cave" as boasted by Lester Howe of his Garden of Eden. Only about a mile away from Howe Caverns, Secret Caverns is an attractive, complex fissure system, typical of New York state caves, with high domes and few formations. A 100-foot waterfall was added to Secret Caverns in the early 1930s; ponded water from the surface is fed into the cave by means of an electric switch. The two caves are not connected, yet share a similar underground drainage system; fluorescent dye has been traced from Secret Caverns to the stream that exits beneath Howe Caverns' old entranceway in the cement quarry.

Secret Caverns, too, has an intriguing history. At the

turn of the century, it was Richtmyer's Cave, which, according to cave explorer/author Clay Perry, the state geologists explored in 1906 and "gave a very discouraging report about."

"It consists of a medium-sized room and a widened joint in Manlius (limestone) which may be followed for 300 feet," the earliest explorers wrote.

Perry continued: "But some roving spelunkers crept into it, and lo and behold: 'We may call this one Nameless cavern, since it was so little known at the time of our first expedition and so fraught with difficulties that its wonders and beauties had been seen by a few, and we know of no other name.

"It is our belief that one of our group, our guide on this trip, was the first to fully explore this cavern."

The "roving spelunkers" were the four-man party organized by Cobleskill historian Arthur VanVoris for his newspaper series and his pamphlet on behalf of the Bright Star Flashlight Company. VanVoris, Edward Rew, and two of the "VanNatten boys" visited the cave in the late months of 1928. In the manuscript that followed the newspaper series, VanVoris wrote: "We understood that it was about to be prepared for a commercial opening, and that the owner did not want any private explorations to be made."

VanVoris felt that the Nameless Cavern was the most fascinating of Schoharie County's lesser caves, and he also described it as being the most extensive. The Cobleskill historian's newspaper report of November 22, 1928, provides a rare description of the cave *before* its development.

Excerpts from the *Cobleskill Times* story by VanVoris and Rew follow.

"The surface entrance is easy—a gradual climb down into a rock hole sufficiently large and with natural cut rock steps for a safe footing.

"Shortly one leaves the light of day behind and by means of flashlights, after climbing down over rocks a bit further, we found a short wood ladder conveniently placed for getting down a fifteen foot ledge.

"Then very soon, there is another drop off which is left behind if the visitor is willing to slide down a pole that had been placed obliquely from the top of this ledge to the floor beneath.

"Continuing down toward the bottom floor of the cavern, progress from this point, without any exaggeration, becomes difficult.

"For the passage from this spot for a distance of many feet is nothing but a crevice through which the visitor must squeeze his way, a few inches at a time, by means of knees and elbows, bearing distinctly in mind the undesirable feature of slipping down through this crevice which yawns beneath his very feet into the depths below.

"A certain presence of mind is essential and progress must be extremely slow, picturing if you can, the visitors wedging themselves forward and down through a crevice so narrow that it is impossible to turn around—face to one rock wall and back to the other and at one particular spot, these walls coming so close together that one almost feels an added inch of breadth would prevent wedging between them.

"Judging from the ladder and pole just mentioned, this part of the cavern and the ensuing two hundred feet or more along the rock floor negotiated by crawling, sliding prone and bending down have been known to numerous previous visitors who have managed the narrow crevices.

"But here is something in the way of an obstacle which may have prevented further progress into the regions beyond, for any who have come to this point without guides to suggest the possibility of passing the obstacle.

"In fact, one of these earlier visitors mentioned to us that he concluded this was the end of possible progress, for at this point the rock wall shelves down to the floor leaving an archway not more than two feet high and three feet wide and the floor of this archway, if we may call it thus, is no longer rock— but water.

"The water is not deep but it is extremely cold and looking ahead with the flashlight, one cannot determine its duration nor possible depth off under the low arch.

"But as most of our party had crawled through on the previous visits, and under the urge of their description of rare and beautiful formations to be seen, we rolled up our sleeves and, bending low, crawled on hands and knees through twenty feet of archway, some of us slipping a little water over the tops of our hip boots, we passed this second hazard of pitch darkness and water.

"One could easily spend a half day in the cavern and then perhaps not see it all, for there are two long passages. Time did not permit us to follow both, but with continuing along the one selected, to its far end at an underground lake, and coming back to the entrance again, more than three hours were consumed, thus indicating something of its size and interest.

"We all estimated that we must have covered well over a mile in distance and we do know that the general direction is south by east, as shown by our compass.

"And our memories do not serve us well enough to attempt any description of the gorgeous sights disclosed to us, in any proper sequence of observing them, so very much did we see and over such a distance covered.

"There are no large amphitheaters like the one in Ball's Cave but there were many high rooms and ceilings so lofty that searchlights did not penetrate the darkness to these heights.

"Many side rooms opened up along the main passage with round and perfectly smooth walls and conical roofs aptly termed 'silos' by some of the party.

"Another spot was called the Rocky Mountains on account of deposits of huge boulders which had to be climbed over, massed up in the passage, twenty or thirty feet high.

"Water was encountered along much of this main passage but at no place to any uncomfortable depth.

"In the high spots, one could walk along just as we are accustomed to do on the ground level. When the ceiling dropped toward floor level, we had to stoop down and in a couple of instances, it was so low that there was no other choice than to lie flat amongst stones, sand and wet gravel and slide along by means of toes and elbows, a few inches at a slide.

"Now and then, the rock floor presented a most unusual appearance, as some of the party remarked, looking exactly like a man-made concrete cellar bottom studded with round stones. One might imagine that at its period of creation, these round stones had been lodged in the softer bottom which had then hardened into a natural sub-base holding them as secure as if set in concrete.

"In the side-wall of one room was a petrified tree stump, hard as flint and yet a stump of a tree as plainly as could be.

"Of the formations which we all like to associate in our minds with caverns, our mere words are so inadequate as to dampen any attempt to tell you about them.

"Those who had gone as far as the water archway, missed all of these formations as they had not formed on the entrance side.

"Soon after this water hazard had been passed, we began to see them—stalactites of all sizes and shapes hanging from the ceiling and stalagmites formed on the floor against the side walls—and so many of them.

"Countless scores and hundreds and to substantiate this statement into an unexaggerated fact, may we remark that they were so abundant that in passing along beneath the low walls, I doubt if there was a single member of the party who's flannel shirt was not pretty well shredded by the time we had gotten back to the entrance after the exploration.

"Stalactites and stalagmites, gray, brown, white, rose-hued—from their special limestone upbuilding.

"Stalagmites weighing several hundred pounds— stalactites as tiny and fragile as a match.

"Solid and everlasting. Slender, graceful, feathery, lacy.

"Coral-like. Smooth and round. Horned. Branched, Conical.

"Here and there along this passage were small grottoes whose entire walls were formed by stalactites growing downward and meeting stalagmites forming up from the floor.

"Now and then, where the roof was low and side walls narrow, these formations were so plentiful, hanging down like pointed horns or rough, coral-like thorns that arms and shoulders were scratched despite the protection of clothing, to say nothing of the rents and tears caused by pushing along, as mentioned a while back.

"It was estimated from the depth at the entrance and the subsequent turnings and windings that this cavern must lie between one hundred and one hundred fifty feet beneath the surface, although no accurate measurement was taken, nor perhaps could be, without a perpendicular opening from the lowest point.

"At the far end of the passage, the roof again shelves down almost to the floor, leaving just enough room to slide along lying flat and wriggling forward foot by foot. After some twenty five feet of such progress, the passage ends at an underground lake and beyond this, it is safe to believe that no man has even passed and so like one of the famous caverns of the Shenandoah Valley, aside from our own appellation of 'Nameless', one might also call it 'Endless.'

"In conclusion, may we remark as previously stated in another article that it has been our good fortune to have, by chance, visited these lesser caverns of Schoharie County exactly according to their size and interest, each one being more fascinating than its predecessor? And in this cavern, one is impelled to leave it with the emotion that he has gazed upon one of the marvels of Nature whose untouched grandeur is such that words alone are utterly inadequate to convey the desired impressions."

Today, Secret Caverns is an aggressive rival and does a modest business during the summer months. The admission price is reasonable, and it is worth a trip. The Mallery family and the Howe Caverns corporation, in which the Mallerys still own stock, are strange bedfellows. Dozens of signs to lure tourists away from Howe to Secret Caverns are permanently in place on Mallery property at the entrance to the grounds of the Howe Caverns estate.

Mallery and his work crews were, for the most part, responsible for the modern look of the Howe Caverns the public sees. Some—but not many—visitors to Howe Caverns have expressed the opinion that the cave has been overly commercialized: an elevator ride for an entrance, clean brick pathways, concealed lighting, and in places, man-made passages. Secret Caverns, while made comfortable for the public, is more of an adventure, as their current billboards promote.

Oddly, Secret Caverns' advertising literature has always subtly criticized the modern engineering developments at Howe and promoted the more natural appeal of the Mallery family's cave. For many years, the billboards for Secret Caverns boasted that the cave's "Natural Entrance Saves You Money"; the brochure noted that "the use of a Natural Entrance makes for such a reasonable admission price, you can't afford to miss a trip through Secret Caverns."

The current brochure notes, "Explorations proved Secret Caverns the most extensive in the Northeast, and they have been retained in their natural state to be enjoyed by people every year from all over the country."

It is interesting to note the changes made over the years in the ways in which the two caverns are presented to the public. Two examples: the Fairyland formations of Secret Caverns became "The City Hit by Atomic Bomb" after World War II. The antiwar, antinuclear-power movement of the 1970s prompted a second name change to "City of the Future." In Howe Caverns, the former Bell of Moscow became "The Giant Beehive" after the tragedy that took the lives of two employees.

Mallery was also manager of the short-lived Schoharie Caverns, located midway between Schoharie and Gallupville. Believed to be opened in September 1935, Schoharie Caverns must have been closed soon after.

According to Schoharie Caverns' advertising circular (which is quite rare):

"Here, unlike the other caverns of Schoharie County, the entrance is located on the side of a mountain.

"The trip starts with a boat ride on an Underground Lake; then one walks through a beautiful winding passageway well decorated with stalactites and stalagmites together with great masses of flowstone such as are found in no other cavern in the North. At the end of the trip, the cavern is blocked by great formations of flowstone hanging down to a deep pool of water.

"Electric lights and board walks, together with the absence of stairs, permit old as well as young to explore this cavern almost without effort. The trip requires about 30 minutes.

"This cavern has been developed to meet the present day demand for a cavern with a low admission fee and at the same time the public is given the opportunity of seeing a cavern which is second to none in the north."

Cave explorer/author Clay Perry reported in the mid-1940s: "This cave was leased and efforts made to enlarge the entrance and some of its passages. . . . After building plank walks and extending electric lines in waterproof cables far inside, the project failed, due to the depression of the 1930s, and the whole thing was abandoned. The walks and cables, light sockets, and a large engine set up on concrete outside, were left to rust and rot."

Over the last six decades, Schoharie Caverns has reverted to its "wild" state. Because its one-half-mile length is mostly walking passage, the cave today is popular among novice cave explorers. Some of the electrical wiring and rotted board walks remained in this popular noncommercial cave up until only about ten years ago. The entrance gate, a wrought-iron spider on its web, still remains.

It is difficult to imagine a boat ride in any portion of Schoharie Caverns, unless the boats were very narrow. In many places the cavern walls close to a width of less than four feet. For most of the 2,000-foot caverns' walking passage, the width is between six and eight feet wide. The water, most of the year, is just ankle deep.

But the admission fee was only thirty-five cents, with special rates for groups of three or more. Children under twelve accompanied by a parent were admitted without charge, according to the advertising literature.

D. C. "Dellie" Robinson had also been involved with the Howe Caverns project, as a surveyor, and is listed as general manager in the caverns' corporation's prospectus.

In 1933—four years after the reopening of Howe's Cave—
Robinson purchased and opened Knox Cave, just outside
of Altamont, in Albany County. He offered both Van Voris
and Colonel Rew the opportunity to join the venture for
$100 each, Robinson seeking to raise $1,000 to "do the
necessary excavating and build the wooden stairs."

Robinson installed staircases and electric lighting and
made other improvements; a combined roller-skating rink
and ticket office was built, and weekly dances at the cave
were well attended through the mid-1950s.

Knox Cave, too, has an interesting history. In 1934,
explorers probing the undeveloped reaches of the cave
found a 2-foot-by-3-foot stone tablet, covered with hieratic
writing, believed to have been left in the cave by the
Iroquois Indians.

On July 31, 1935, the *Albany Evening News* carried the
following report, under the headline "Visitors to Knox
Cave Find Huge Tooth on Rocky Floor."

"KNOX—Dancers gathered for the semi-weekly
'squares' at the Knox Cave dancing pavilion near here
last Saturday night decided to enter the cave before
the orchestra tuned up for the evening, and by so
doing made a new discovery.

"It is in the form of a huge tooth in excellent
condition, which has been submitted to geologists
and paleontologists at the State Department of Education for a verdict as to its original owner.

"The tooth, found near the spring, remote from
the entrance to the cave, was evidently washed clear
of the shale debris from overhead. The management
of the cave is anxiously awaiting word from the
Albany scientists to which it has been submitted."

Knox is an extensive cave system. Robinson spent two decades trying to prove that it was the largest cave in the northeast, according to the 1976 guide *Caves of Albany County, NY.* In the mid- to late 1950s, several discoveries more than doubled the cave's known length at that time, to more than 3,000 feet. Until the roller-skating rink burned and Knox Cave closed in 1958, Robinson had a standing agreement with cave explorers to waive the fifty-cent admission fee, and he offered a $100 reward to any group making additional discoveries.

In 1975, an ice fall in the Knox Cave entrance sinkhole killed one cave explorer and injured another. The cave is now closed and gated.

9

The Legacy of Lester Howe

THE LEGACY OF LESTER HOWE: THE "LOST" GARDEN OF EDEN CAVE

The legend of Lester Howe's lost Garden of Eden cave, "bigger and better" than his first, continues to confound modern folk historians and the active band of cave explorers who enjoy their sport in the cavern-rich hills of Schoharie County.

Extensive efforts to find the purported underground legacy of Lester Howe followed the reopening of his "first cave." Several interesting finds were reported and publicized.

And the search continues. Since Howe's death in 1888, more than 150 Schoharie County caves have been found and explored—most of them small, wet, and miserable; most barely large enough to crawl into. With some possible exceptions: VanVliet's Cave, just outside the Village of Schoharie; Sitzer's Cave, about two miles east of Howe's

Garden of Eden farm property; Secret Caverns, the commercialized competitor; the Sinks by the Sugarbush, and McFail's Cave, both to the northwest of Howe Caverns. But none to compare with Howe.

Lieutenant Colonel Edward A. Rew, a Cobleskill postal employee who accompanied his friend Arthur VanVoris on many of his expeditions for the unpublished manuscript *Lesser Caverns of Schoharie County*, claimed to have found the Garden of Eden by following a mysterious "Finger of Geology."

In 1950, in a letter to Clay Perry, author of *Underground Empire*, Rew described his 1931 explorations in a Schoharie Cave that he took the liberty of renaming "Rew Caverns." Excerpts from the letter, which accompanied an article Perry had authored on the legendary lost cavern for the Cobleskill weekly newspaper, follow:

"The cave I wanted to tell you about, 'Rew Caverns', is not located anywhere near the recent explorations of the Garden of Eden Cave, although I believe they are one and the same cave. . . .

"I went many times [to the Howe's farm property] by myself, and in sitting on the rock ledges, noted that you could see across the valley many places where Howe Caverns had exits on different levels into the valley, all of which pointed in the general direction of the Garden of Eden.

BARN HIDES ENTRANCE

"I also noticed that Mr. Howe had built his barn at the very edge of a cliff and had brought shale rock from across his land a good 200 yards to fill for a barnyard. . . . It became my belief that this barnyard hides the entrance to the cavern he spoke of, or at least it was his intention to make people think that it did."

After talking with elderly local residents, Colonel Rew wrote, in his letter to Perry:

"I came to the conclusion that Howe was an honest man and that he had undoubtedly found a cavern which was bigger and better than his original exploration. I realized that alone, I could not dig away the shale that made the barnyard.

"At about this time, a gentleman from Schoharie came to Arthur [Van Voris] with the story that he had a small cave over on the bank of the Schoharie River and wanted us to come over and look at it. We went into this small cave for a short distance to where we came to a water crawl, the conditions were such that although it was four or five feet wide, the water was eight or ten inches deep and the roof of the cave about the same distance from the water, which would necessitate crawling through and holding the light in your teeth.

"For some reason or other, I didn't feel like going through it at the time. . . . Late in the Fall of the same year, I was home going over my cave records and on consulting the map, suddenly realized that the show of exits on the north of the Cobleskill Valley made by Howe Caverns, the Garden of Eden, and this small cave on the banks of the Schoharie River all lined up.

"I, of course, came to the conclusion that the Cobleskill Valley was geologically a much newer valley than the Schoharie and that originally the caves that are now known as Secret and Howe Caverns extended on through to the Schoharie River and that the digging of the Cobleskill Valley had cut this cave in two ... and that in all probability the small cave we had explored on the Schoharie river bank was a side passage from the lower end of this cavern.

"I went over at once to the cavern, and went through the water hole and found a tremendous cavern. I explored this cavern not much over half a mile back of the general direction of the Garden of Eden and was stopped by a cliff which undoubtedly was formerly a waterfall, at least 30 feet high, and which could not be scaled by a person alone. The cavern was so high that the beam of my flashlight could not reach the ceiling.

"It's beautiful in formations, the cliff being completely covered with flowstone. One interesting note that in this cavern I found the only crystal formation I have ever seen in the caverns of Schoharie County."

In the close of his letter, Rew explains why he decided to wait nearly twenty years before coming forward with this information.

"After this partial exploration, I had the choice of getting help to complete the exploration and therby letting the world know of my discovery, or keeping quiet and respecting the memory of Lester Howe's secret, who was probably the only other person to see this cavern. I decided that it was much more fun to keep quiet, letting only Arthur know that I had made a discovery, without giving him any ideas as to how I gained my entrance."

Rew's Caverns is believed by most to be one and the

same as VanVliet's Cave along the Schoharie Creek. Later explorers have been unable to follow the Colonel's lead.

In his book *Depths of the Earth*, William R. Halliday, M.D., director of the Western Speleological Society, researched additional claims made by Rew to the editor of the *Cobleskill Times:*

"[The Garden of Eden cave] is richer and more spectacular than any hitherto unexplored cavern in Schoharie County, or, for that matter, any other in the North. I personally and alone, on a secret expedition, discovered and explored it one night in 1931 to the extent of about two miles.

"The Finger of Geology points to the Garden of Eden Cave. Read the geology and keep at it, and you'll find it just as I did!" Rew boasted.

Halliday continued:

"At various times, Colonel Rew happily planted intentionally puzzling hints. Some may have been red herrings. Often he referred to the geological structure of Terrace Mountain, southeast across the valley from Howe Caverns. On occasion he mentioned the relative ages of nearby valleys.... He hinted broadly that he had forced a seasonal siphon [a place where the water meets the ceiling of a cave, blocking further passage] in little VanVliet's Cave."

Rew's claims have yet to be substantiated, and Rew died in Little Rock, Arkansas, in January 1978. Many believe his claim to be a hoax.

If the lost Garden of Eden Cave was on or near Howe's property of the same name, Sitzer's Cave, on Terrace Mountain, would be the logical contender. Sitzer's Cave, about two miles northeast from the former Howe farm property, was the object of extensive search and speculation during the late 1940s by an Oneonta caving club.

Sitzer's looks promising. In spring, and after heavy rains, a powerful underground stream floods from the small entrance, indicating a cave of considerable potential.

Mr. Sitzer, the owner of the property, reported that he had been in the cavern for some distance and "had seen some remarkable, larger chambers." But in or about 1929, Sitzer told the explorers, "an earth shock started a huge landslide that completely buried the entrance...with thousands of tons of rock and earth."

In 1948, the Tri-County Grotto of the National Speleological Society tried to reopen Sitzer's Cave. Their efforts were publicized by author Clay Perry in a Cobleskill newspaper article. Perry wrote that the group "succeeded in digging and blasting away enough of the landslide to drain a large underground lake to a considerable extent, lowering its level, they say, about 15 feet.... Some of them wormed their way in and found a large chamber and reported another beyond where they could get to, but said the water must be further lowered before more progress could be made."

Further explorations in Sitzer's Cave have yielded little. A 1966 guide to the caverns of Schoharie County provides the following description: "The cave consists of several rooms that are connected by very wet crawlways. The cave can be entered for 140 feet to a point where the ceiling almost comes to the water. The passage continues and could be followed even further if the water level ever falls, even by a few inches."

Another claim to the Garden of Eden was fired off in 1929 as the first salvo in the battle for the tourist dollar between Howe Caverns, Inc., and its neighbor/competitor, Secret Caverns.

Less than three months after the reopening of Howe

Caverns, the former Nameless Cavern was officially christened Secret Caverns and opened to the public. In announcements to the press, Mallery said he decided on the name because of the cavern Lester Howe had kept secret. The August 15, 1929, *Cobleskill Times* reported: "It is believe that this is the subterranean wonder which Howe had in mind at that time."

It is possible, but not likely. Less than a mile to the northeast of Howe Caverns, Mallery's cavern is a tight yet long fissure cave, with high domes and a small, active stream. There are few formations. The cavern is young, according to its owners, formed during the great Ice Age 10,000 years ago. It just doesn't fit Howe's description of the Garden of Eden cave.

Yet Secret Caverns is an extensive cave system, with some intriquing possibilities. A narrow, tortuous connection beyond the 100-foot waterfall on the tourist route has been found to link Secret Caverns and Benson's Cave to the east. The double cave extends in the form of an inverted V, to account for more than one-half mile of cave passage. Just 2,500 feet to the south, the water from the Secret-Benson system emerges in Baryte's Cave.

The highway that approaches Howe Caverns and Secret Caverns is lined with billboards. It is easy to understand the commonly asked question, "Are the two caves connected?" The answer is no, and yes.

The entrance to Baryte's Cave is through the original entrance to Howe's Cave, now in the abandoned quarry of the North American Cement Company.

In 1904, mining broke through a small crawl space in the caverns' floor and uncovered a strange phenomenon: two caves, each with its own underground stream, one stream crossing the other, and until then, unconnected.

Baryte's Cave, of which more than a quarter mile has been explored, heads to the north in the direction of the Secret-Benson system. Making a physical connection of the three caverns would yield a bigger (longer), cave, but not a better one. Linking the Baryte's-Secret-Benson Cave system to the original Howe's Cave would be an impressive cavern by any standard.

There is another, long-standing rumor of a connection between Howe Caverns and its competitor. A tight, tortuous crawlway, Fat Man's Misery, extends Howe Caverns beyond the Winding Way at the cave's northernmost point and again heads in the direction of Secret Caverns. Fat Man's Misery (as this entire section of the cave has come to be known) has been explored to a length of more than 1,800 feet and continues. From the Secret Caverns end, it was reported: "Men who discovered and explored Secret Caverns long before it was commercialized claim that there is another long passage somewhere near the entrance that runs all the way through Howe Caverns. . . . This has been walled up by the owners of Secret Caverns."

Howe Caverns, to this day, remains partially unexplored. The passage through Fat Man's Misery, off the commercial tour, has long been known (since the mid-1800s), and early tours ventured along it by oil lamp as far as the 50-foot-high Ramsey's Rotunda. The explored passage continues for about another tortuous 1,000 feet of backbreaking stooping, walking, and crawling through icy 42-degree water. In most places, the ceiling is less than four feet high. Until the 1950s, explorers stopped at this point. On the first modern maps of Howe Caverns, displayed at the lodge entrance for tourists, the passage is referred to as the Lake of Mystery, On Which No Man Has Ever Sailed.

Beyond The Lake of Mystery is Reynold's River, named

Top, THE ORIGINAL OR NATURAL ENTRANCE TO HOWES CAVE—An early woodcut of the "Blowing Rock" published in 1843 for the state survey, *Geology of New York. Bottom*, WASHINGTON'S HALL—From the Stoddard series, copyright 1889. This portion of the cave no longer exists; it was destroyed by mining operations in the Howes Cave cement quarry. *(Photos courtesy of Howe Caverns, Inc.)*

WEDDING IN THE BRIDAL CHAMBER OF THE "OLD CAVE"—Believed by many to be the September, 1854, wedding of Harriet Elgiva Howe and Hiram Shipman Dewey. If taken in 1854, it is among the earliest photographs taken anywhere in the world with artificial lighting. It would also be the oldest example of cave photography. Photo historians doubt the picture's authenticity, and clothing experts of the period place the date around 1870. Whoever the early publicists were, they went to considerable effort to duplicate the actual Howe-Dewey wedding in the cave. Although the face is partially hidden, the father of the bride looks much like Lester Howe.

(Photo courtesy of Howe Caverns, Inc.)

UNDERGROUND BOATING and the
natural pillar on the Lagoon of
Venus, from a postcard printed
in the early 1930s.

VIRGIL CLYMER—A Syracuse attorney, Clymer was instrumental
in the formation of the caverns'
corporation, fund raising and pro-
motion.
(Photo courtesy of Howe Caverns, Inc.)

THE AUTHOR, WET AND MISERABLE, crawling through 42-degree water in the section of cave beyond the Giant Rotunda.
(Photo by Bob Addis)

THROUGH FAT MAN'S MISERY—Cave Explorer Bob Addis squeezes through "Fat Man's Misery" to enter the section of cave beyond the commercial tour.
(Photo by the author)

for a former manager at the cave. Reynold's River enters the undeveloped cave at about 800 feet into the passage and soon disappears behind a pile of collapsed limestone ceiling. From there, the passage "goes" (in cave jargon) —becoming increasingly tighter. Explorers can stand in places, the walls of the cave pressing against their chests. It continues northward, passing under the fields of the Sagendorf farm, toward the Secret Caverns entrance lodge.

It wasn't until 1975 that four caverns guides—the author, Steve Crum, Chris Walsh, and John Clark—and Bob Addis, a former guide, pushed on beyond this point, continuing in the direction of Secret Caverns. Wearing wetsuits and protective clothing, with hardhats and miners' lamps for light, Addis and Crum pushed this undeveloped section of the Winding Way to its reasonable limits. At that point, another 700 feet from the end of Reynold's River, the narrow cave passage is blocked by a deep pool which meets the cave ceiling. Above it is loose rockfall. But it continues—unexplored, despite our attempts to reach the passage's end.

Connecting the upper and lower ends of Howe Caverns to Secret Caverns through the Winding Way (upper) and Baryte's Cave (lower) passages would create the northeast's most extensive cave system. Mapped, the system would resemble an italicized pound sign, or #.

Another possible Garden of Eden was explored in the late 1950s, and it, too, was not far from Howe Caverns. By coincidence, it was owned by the VanNatten family. Jim VanNatten, a former Howe Caverns tour guide, nearly lost his life in a freak accident at the cave in 1930.

The entrance pit of the Sinks by the Sugarbush is in the dense maple woods just northeast of Howe. There, explorers from Albany came upon perhaps the most exciting find to date in the search for the legendary Garden of Eden: nineteenth-century artifacts from Lester Howe's collection.

In an article on the Garden of Eden mystery, Clay Perry wrote in the *Cobleskill Times:* "An astonishing find was made in the VanNatten cavern, a pair of oriental bronzes which are believed to be arabian hookahs or water pipes, and perhaps adapted to use as oil lamps. They bore the crudely scratched initials of 'L.H.' and the date, '1845.' These are believed to be of Indonesian or Arabian origin, dating back before the Christian era, and perhaps brought to this country by some sea-captain, who made port at Hudson when it was a whaling port. And that Lester Howe gained possession of them and took them into this cavern, for what purpose can only be surmised."

But the Sinks by the Sugarbush cavern is impassable. Over time, the tight entrance pit has become plugged with fallen rocks and debris. If a bigger and better cave continues beyond the drop, it cannot be reached without drastic measures, or explosives. And the date, 1845, would have been just three years after the discovery of Howe's "first cave." It seems reasonable to assume Howe would have had no reason to plot his subtle revenge at such an early date.

There is some discrepancy in the historical records of the explorations of the caves in the Carlisle Center area, which lies to the northeast of Howe Caverns. Two caves, McFail's and Selleck's, were explored during the 1840s; the initials of T. N. McFail and the date 1844 are near the bottom of the entrance shaft of Selleck's Cave.

McFail's Cave is the only cavern found, to date, that could .in any respect be considered "bigger and better" than Howe's.

Descriptions of the McFail's and Selleck's caves from the

mid-1800s are confusing. Until the early 1960s, both caves were regarded as pretty but very small, with each having a small lake just off the entrance pit. But rumors from the turn of the century persisted—a stream passage, indicating more cave, extended northeast/southwest, the stream running southwest: in the direction of Howe Caverns! But in which cave was it, McFail's—or Selleck's Cave, where McFail's initials were found?

At the turn of the century, a systematic search in the Loesser's woods area of Carlisle Center led to the discovery and exploration of Cave Disappointment. In the early 1950s, three new vertical caves were found in the same area and named (quite colorfully) after their discoverers: Hanor's Cave, Ack's Shack, and Featherstonehaugh's Flop.

It wasn't until 1960 that a cave matching the description of McFail's was found, only about 200 feet to the northeast of Ack's Shack. With a great deal of pushing—a cavers' term for physically forcing one's body through tight, tortuous cave passages—McFail's Hole was dangerous. The area around the entrance was crumbling and filling with debris. Persistent explorers squeezed almost one-half mile of treacherous passage from McFail's "Hole"—hardly descriptive of a "Garden of Eden." In 1961, Fred Stone of Cornell University crawled, literally with his nose to the ceiling, through a tight, nearly water-filled passage with only about two inches of breathing space. He emerged into the main portion of McFail's Cave, now the largest in the Northeast. Continuous explorations in McFail's Cave over the last two decades have yielded nearly five miles of underground passages, much of it large walking passage like the commercialized section of Howe Caverns. The cave is dangerous, and in parts unstable. A trespassing explorer lost his life climbing from the entrance pit in

1968, a victim of exposure. The McFail's Hole entrance has collapsed completely; entrance is now through either Ack's Shack or Hall's Hole, the latter discovered only recently.

If McFail's cave is the legendary Garden of Eden, we must consider Lester Howe a very courageous man—or very foolhardy—when weighing the risks modern explorers have taken to push McFail's to its reputed status as "bigger and better." It is unlikely Howe took similar risks, considering his age at the time, and the primitive cave-exploring tools and methods of the late 1800s. Unless, of course, there was another, less difficult entrance into the cave.

Because of its sensitive environment (McFail's is home to thousands of endangered bats) and its unique place in New York speleology, McFail's Cave is owned and protected by the National Speleological Society. All entrances to the cave are locked and gated. Trespassing signs are posted prominently.

McFail's Cave also passes another "test" of Garden of Eden status. The main cave passage of McFail's follows a northwest/southeast fault line that is believed to be directly aligned with the fault-controlled passages of Howe Caverns, less than two impenetrable miles apart. The Sinks by the Sugarbush are along the same fault. Line-drawn maps of the passages of Howe Caverns can be said to resemble a right hand with the index finger outstretched. Could this be the mysterious "Finger of Geology?

But the finger points in the opposite direction, following the supposed fault line to the southeast leads to VanVliet's Cave. And geologists have surmised that VanVliet's was cut off eons ago from a massive cave corridor (of which Howe and McFail's were a part) by two glacial river valleys and Terrace Mountain. If the mysterious "Finger of Geology" points to VanVliet's Cave, as Colonel Rew suggested, there's much more to the cave than modern explorers have been able to crawl their way into.

The mystery remains unsolved, and so the search for the Garden of Eden cave continues. Interest was again piqued in the late 1970s, when construction of Interstate 88 was underway. Explosives blasted the east-west route through the northern section of the county, and there were continuous rumors of the work crews finding gaping holes in the hillsides and of drills being lost in bottomless pits. Harrison Terk, the general manager of Howe Caverns, reports workers dumped 80 tons of rock into a large sinkhole on or near the former Howe farm. Additionally, two small caves were exposed just across the valley from the old entrance to Howe's Cave. Located at the top of the escarpment, these two lesser caverns are clearly visible from the I-88 highway.

If the Garden of Eden cavern was on Howe's property, the cave is gone forever: there are four lanes of new highway directly over the former home of the great cave explorer and developer.

Did the Garden of Eden ever exist? Or did Howe, an aged and bitter old man, create the myth to confound those who he felt had swindled him from his property? Only Howe could say for certain.

It should be noted that for all their seeming permanence, caves *do* change. Spring floods fill once-open passages with clay, mud, and debris; surface and subsurface erosion take their toll, and weeds, brush, and vines cover once-visible entranceways. The undeveloped Fat Man's Misery section of Howe Caverns is filled with sand and clay from Spring flooding almost every year. When the crawlway was reopened in May 1988, and photographed for this book, eager explorers hauled more than sixty fifty-pound feed sacks of earth from the passage, which is only about 30 feet long.

The search for the Garden of Eden has continued for just over a century since the death of Lester Howe. It is just as likely that the search will continue for again as long, and new explorers will proclaim its discovery.

And perhaps there really is a Garden of Eden cavern, larger and more magnificent than world-famous Howe Caverns. Perhaps in the future, a team of explorers will push their way into a small, tight crawlway that had been previously overlooked, or stumble upon a hidden cave entrance somewhere in the deep woods. There, in a vast room miles into the hillside, set among abundant crystalline formations, the explorers may find carved in the limestone wall, or written in soot from an oil-burning lamp:

Garden of Eden Cave, Discovered 1873. L. Howe

10

Modern History

By the time of the caverns' reopening in 1929, the Howe family had long since moved from the area. But many of Lester Howe's descendants continued to show considerable interest in the cave over the years, and they maintain a great sense of family pride in its discovery. It is rare when during the course of the year at least one distant relative does not tour Howe Caverns.

Helen Howe, a broadway showgirl, and great-grand-daughter of Lester's brother, Elmon, married Anthony Gianelli of Schenectady in the Bridal Altar of the caverns in December 1929. It was the fourth cave wedding.

Four years later, in September 1933, Howe's great-grand-nephew, Herbert Howe, of Schenectady, was married in the cave to Rose Gardner, of Middleburgh.

For many years, one of the most prized possessions held

by the family was the guest register from the Cave House Hotel. The register, which covers the years from 1844 to 1855, was presented in 1965 to the Schoharie County Historical Society by Howe's great-granddaughters.

In written remarks for the presentation, Frances Howe Miller recalled:

"Our grandmother, and our mother, Annie Laurie Dewey Miller, both delighted in this book. I recall from childhood the family dinner parties which we were invited to at our grandmother's home in Jefferson City, Missouri. . . .

"She [Harriet Howe Dewey] used to get out what we called her 'Cave Book' and read to us the most interesting entries, especially the various poems which gave her particular pleasure."

In his pamphlet history of the Howe family, Warren Howe writes:

"A family story related in 1985 by Helen Howe Gianelli told of an incident which occurred when a noted scientist, author, and explorer visited the cave. With 'great flourish and cameras . . . he made an exploration.' At a subsequent college lecture he told of the wonders of Howe's Cave and described how far he had gone into it. 'He said it wasn't safe to go farther without scaffolding.' Helen's grandfather, Samuel, then a young boy, laughed at the scientist's claim: 'Why, I have been there much farther,' and told his father, Elmon Howe, about the 'water and bright stones further back in the cave.'"

In the late summer of 1954, the caverns' general manager, Howard Hall, received a letter from the wife of Howe's grandson, Mrs. Charles E. Dewey. Her husband's parents were Hiram and Harriet (Howe) Dewey, married in the caverns' Bridal Chamber more than a century earlier. It was published on the front page of the *Cobleskill Index* on August 5:

DAUGHTER OF LESTER HOWE WAS MARRIED IN NEARBY CAVERNS A CENTURY AGO

Dear Sir:

September twenty-seventh of this year will be the one-hundredth anniversary of the marriage of my husband's parents in what was then known as the Bridal Chamber of Howe's Cave. We had hoped to be there for a celebration, but it looks as though we shall not make it. However, I thought as a matter of interest to visitors you would like to choose some items from data which I can supply.

The bride was Elgiva, one of the two daughters of Lester Howe, owner of the Cave. She was small and retiring with blue eyes and an abundance of light brown hair. The groom, whose name is tucked away inconspicuously in a corner of the invitation to the wedding reception, was six feet tall, handsome and fun-loving, with dark brown hair and deep blue eyes. However, Mr. Hiram Shipman Dewey was a person of importance even then, being a civil engineer engaged in railroad work. He had worked for the Saratoga and Whitehall, the Whitehall and Rutland, the Harlem Extension and later for the Albany and Susquehanna and the Schenectady and Athens railroads. He made the first surveys for the Westshore from Hoboken to Newburgh and in 1859 and 1860 he was chief engineer for the New York and Connecticut boundary commission. He made a survey of the entire line, located and erected all the monuments and his work was confirmed by the legislature of both states, whereas previous surveys had been condemned. In 1865 he went to Kentucky and supervised the building of a hundred and forty miles of railroad. Three years later he went to Springfield, Illinois to be with the Wabash Railroad and in the fall of 1878 located in Jefferson City, Mo. He had left construction work in twenty-one states and had spent three years on the Pacific coast.

We visited the cave back in the rubber boot and torch days and regret that we have not been able to enjoy all the wonderful improvements you have made. We congratulate you upon improving and preserving the site and wish you the best of luck always.

Cordially yours,
Anne Stuart Dewey
(Mrs. Charles E.)
Holts Summit, MO

P.S. Mother went with her daughter back to the scene of her wedding in 1904. My husband remembers visiting there when he was a little boy and seeing his grandfather stand in the boat while crossing the lake and strike the "harp" with his cane.

The one millionth visitor to Howe Caverns was Caroline Miskimen, of Philadelphia, who toured the cave on June 28, 1948. Amid the massive publicity effort, Mrs. Miskimen was interviewed in the cave on WGY radio, and received an 8,000-year-old stalagmite mounted on a mahogany base with inlaid cave "pearls." She was also presented with a copy of Clay Perry's *Underground Empire* autographed by the author.

Despite its 150-year history, there was little accurate scientific data collected on the famous cave until after the turn of the twentieth century.

Before that time, a distinction between the works of God and the natural sciences was unclear in the public mind. Nineteenth-century scientists had formulated numerous rudimentary theories on the natural processes, and many of these theories were later proved to contain at least some element of scientific truth. But by and large, the American public still held to their belief that the Heavenly Creator was directly responsible for crafting the great geologic works of nature. Advertising material from as late as the 1890s referred to the cave's formation as "a wonderful creation and an interesting study for those who adore the Great Author of the Universe, and delight in contemplating His wonderous works." Yet as early as 1846, a visit to Howe's Cave could plant the seeds of religious doubt. "There creeps unbidden into the mind a vague and indefinite idea that [the cave's] vast proportions must have required ages on ages, more than 6,000 years, in their formation," wrote one early visitor. He referred to the commonly held belief among believers in the literal truth of the Bible that the world was only 6,000 years old.

Yet by coincidence, it was a religious man, the Reverend Horace Hovey, who published what could be called the first scientific analysis of Howe's Cave. Hovey visited the cave in 1880 with his son; their findings, along with reports on Mammoth, Luray, and Wyandotte caverns, were published as *Celebrated American Caves*, a first in its field.

While the reverend's geologic report on Howe's Cave was not finely detailed, Hovey wrote that the area's underlying limestone bedrock was "easily acted upon by the elements." The introduction to his chapter on Howe's Cave notes:

"The most massive and prominent rocks in Schoharie county, N.Y., are first, the Water limestones, then the Pentamerus limestone, and above the Delthyris shale. These all belong to the Helderberg division of the Silurian system.... These formations are so related to each other as to favor the excavation of deep valleys, flanked by cliffs and mural escarpments, the hills rising by successive terraces to mountainous proportions. Several caves [have] been found in this region."

Howe's Cave, he concluded, "is one of the largest in the country excavated from the rocks of the Silurian period."

Hovey also produced the first accurate survey and map of Howe's Cave. Because portions of the cave have since been destroyed by quarrying, Hovey's map remains the most accurate historic record of Howe Caverns in its entirety.

Cave maps are useful tools to the speleologists, particularly when used to determine relations with the surrounding surface area. Several maps of Howe Caverns have been updated and revised, often in conjunction with papers presented on the cave geology of Schoharie County and surrounding areas.

Speleology, the study of caves, is a relatively new field of geology. The national constitution of the National Speleological Society was ratified by author Clay Perry and others in Pettibone Falls Cave, in Massachusetts, on December 1, 1940.

Howe Caverns is located in what is referred to by speleologists as an area of "karst topography." In a karst area, surface water drains underground into numerous sinkholes, crevices, and depressions. The Helderberg division, which the Reverend Hovey described, is a regional name given to the underlying belt of limestone, an easily eroded remnant of an ocean bed that existed more than 435 million years ago.

Geologists say that as sediment accumulated, the ocean

floor compressed into solid rock from the weight of successive deposits, and the continents rose gradually over eons of time. The ancient ocean was filled with life—corals, sponges, and shelled animals in many ways similar to the clams, oysters, and snails of today. Their shells, or armor, were built from calcium carbonate, which is now easily identified as the major element of limestone.

From these characteristics, modern speleologists have identified in Howe Caverns three types of limestone, representing two different periods of time in the history of this ancient sea: the Silurian and Devonian ages. Beneath the hills of Howe Caverns country is a bed of limestone that formed during the Silurian age, about 435 million years ago, and the Devonian time period, of about 396 million years ago.

The cave, of course, is much younger, formed by the erosive process of water, beginning only between 5 and 10 million years ago. The ever-present underground stream, the River Styx, courses its way southeasterly today through Howe Caverns, having eroded through successive layers of Coeymans, Manlius, and Roundout limestones.

Most of Schoharie County's cave systems are carved out of the more easily eroded Manlius limestone, of which the major corridors of Howe Caverns are built. According to the *Schoharie County Guide*, "the Manlius is thin-bedded, dark blue limestone of fairly pure composition. The layers are 1 to 3 inches thick, and often alternate dark and light beds. The thin-bedded character of the rock is extremely favorable to the passage of underground water." Although rare in Howe Caverns, the Manlius limestone is said to be rich in fossils.

Early visitors to the cave were enthralled with the cavern's acoustic characteristics. Of the Manlius, the county guide to caves notes, "When struck with a hammer it emits a ringing sound."

The ceiling in the cave is capped by the bluish-grey Coeymans limestone, described by geologists as rather coarse, composed of fossilized fragments of shells, crinoids, and stems. A guide to the area's caves states: "Although caves in the Coeyman's are uncommon, it frequently contains sink-holes and shafts to the Manlius below. The cliffs of the Coeyman's are almost everywhere visible in the region."

The original, natural entrance to the cave, at the cavern's lowest point, is carved from the Roundout limestone, "a thin-bedded, drab-colored lime mud rock."

Although these geological features are not described by the caverns' tour guides, astute visitors to the cave today can spot the point of contact between the Coeyman's and Manlius limestones as they descend the stairs at the base of the elevator shaft; the Manlius caps the Roundout limestone in the deeper section of the cave, near the underground boat ride.

The cave—that hollow cavity within the limestone walls— began to form after the Cretaceous period, some 65 to 136 million years ago, when the North American continent began to rise slowly out of the sea. Rains fell; some drained off in brooks and rivers, some found its way below ground, seeping into the limestone. Taking the path of least resistance, these underground streams followed natural cracks, fault lines, and fissures below the earth.

Speleologists have found evidence in Howe Caverns of two types of water erosion, phreatic and vadose. Pockets of water accumulating below the water table slowly erode into domes and chambers through the phreatic process. This explains the formation of domes and other pockmarks in the caverns ceiling. As the water table lowers, an active stream finds its way underground, often connecting the chambers to form a master cave system. This is known as vadose erosion.

Once the caverns chambers are open, formations—stalactites, stalagmites, flowstone, and other varieties—begin to develop, at the incredibly slow rate of about one cubic inch every 85 to 100 years. Cave formations develop similarly to the way icicles are formed. Rain water seeps through the soil above, dissolving small amounts of limestone in the process. As these drops of water filter through the caverns' roof, the water evaporates and leaves behind tiny particles of a slightly altered limestone, calcite, on the rock surface.

The formations hanging from the ceiling are known as stalactites. Stalagmites, the formations that grow up from the cavern floor, are formed in the same way. Often they are found directly below stalactites and result from drops that fell to the floor before evaporating. Flowstone is formed in the same manner, but the water evaporates as it flows down the cavern walls.

An early view of the caverns' geology was prepared in 1936 for the corporation's *Story of Howe Caverns*, by Professor Harold O. Whitnall, former head of the Department of Geology and Geography of nearby Colgate University. Professor Whitnall was eloquent in his praise of the caverns' beauty. For visitors, he concluded:

"The memory of the underground world lingers. New conceptions of time and law and beauty are theirs. Inspiration comes to many to learn more of the marvels of geology, but aside from scientific zest and philosophic meditations there remains for all the dream picture of a crystal palace like unto one that Pluto may have built for his stolen bride, Persephone."

II

A Romantic Trip

"A ROMANTIC TRIP"

"Underneath a peaceful hillside
   Green with meadow, glade, and tree
Nature's hand has fashioned caverns—
   Wonders that we now may see.

"Rippling water courses through them,
   Chambers clothed in shadows deep,
Domes and archways now awakened
   From a million years of sleep."

—P. L. Thomson, from *Story of Howe
Caverns*, copyright 1936 by Howe Caverns,
Inc.

Today, Lester Howe would hardly recognize his cave. It is well lit with clean brick walks. The caverns' original entrance now stands alone in an abandoned cement quarry, and about 300 feet of his "old cave" have been destroyed. A 156-foot elevator descent takes visitors through the man-made "back door" of the caverns; tourists see little more than a half-mile of the old Howe's Cave.

The public presentation of Howe Caverns is largely the work of local historian Chauncey Rickard, who wrote the tour guides' spiel for the caverns' reopening in 1929. Drawing upon his knowledge of Greek mythology, Rickard named many of the points of interest in the caverns, and wrote the fanciful descriptions of them.

Rickard stood well over six feet, and weighed in the area of two hundred pounds plus. He was much admired by those who knew him, and it is unfortunate that by today's standards, his original writings seem melodramatic to the point of being humorous.

Imagine the reaction of visitors today to Rickard's description of the boat ride and underground lake:

"You have long ago left the familiar world behind. You have brought here nothing from it save memory, and you are now ready to embark on this beautiful fairy sheet of water and ride out into the abode of Gods of Legend and mythology.

"I now summon Vestal and Vulcan to come forth with their fires and light the waters of enchantment, the Lagoon of the priestess of beauty, Venus.

"You now see the blue light of Vestal, soon to be followed by Vulcan the God of fire who floods the realm with vast sparks, as it were, from his ancient anvil. (The boat now leaves the dock.) Here on the left is the statue of Memnon, whose armor was made by Vulcan.

"We now enter the Hall of Adonis, a choice portion of the lagoon, for here Venus has been lavish with her beauty. It is the hall of the beloved youth, Adonis, who, when killed in the chase, the goddess sprinkled nectar into his blood from which flowers sprang up. The ceiling of the abode of Adonis is encrusted with formations typifying the flowers which sprang from this beautiful votive.

"On the left is the dark abode of the vanished Gods from whose spirits Zeus has turned his face, and ahead on the right now appears the mountain and castles of Valhalla, the abode of the ancient warriors who fell on the battlefield fighting bravely. It would seem that here Venus welcomed those warriors from the northland, for the beauty of the world of myth became hers.

"Directly ahead you see a massive pillar of Hercules, dividing the lagoon into two parts. At the base of the pillar is the little bay or cove of Alcestis, whom the mighty Hercules brought back from hell.

(The boat now reverses its course).

"On your right is the arm of Hercules, mutilated, yet powerful in its ruin."

"Looking ahead, there now appears the Ramparts of the Elysium where repose the spirits of the virtuous Gods. The boat is now entering a series of rocky cloisters. Note the Cathedral-like contour of these rocky vaults. Through an almost perfect arch is seen another view, the majestic organ."

Rickard was prolific. He even wrote poems on his employers' behalf.

> In the land of the falling waters
>   Where bride-white birches sway
> Is a cavern of rarest beauty
>   I fain would see some day.

It has tunneled the rocky hillside
To hide a jeweled stream,
For beneath the tall oak and summack
Its tideless currents gleam.

—from "The Marvelous Howe Caverns" souvenir photo album, published in the early 1930s.

The spiel has become less dramatic over the years, and there are many formations in the cave to which Rickard gave a name, but are no longer part of the one-hour-and-fifteen-minute tour. To Rickard's credit, the names of the caverns' current points of interest have remained largely the same; and the story is told only slightly differently.

The cave tour is difficult to describe in words alone. Virgil Clymer, the caverns' first general manager and an attorney by trade, did a pretty good job of it for the *Story of Howe Caverns*, writing:

"Howe Caverns is a type of its own—just as Nature made it. It differs radically from other caverns, being a beautiful canyon made two hundred feet below the surface by an underground stream. For more than a mile the visitor winds his way through Caverns high and wide in which he finds a beautiful lake, galleries, and halls. There are few experiences more fascinating than standing in one of the great chambers and viewing the mysterious, beautiful, and colorful stalactites, stalagmites, and rock creations looming like spectral giants or flaring in delicate veils like floating fairies' wings.

"Two modern elevators descend one hundred and fifty-six feet, noiselessly and with almost imperceptible motion, from the floor of the lodge to the Vestibule of the caverns—a large circular rock-bound room—where the underground trip begins. The purity of the air is at once a subject of comment. The daily temperature is practically uniform at 52° to 56°F. regardless of the extreme of heat or cold at the surface.

"Passing through the portal down a gentle incline, the first stalagmites are seen. They are cone-shaped and of a beautiful bronze tint. Next is a view of the River Styx, two hundred feet below the Lodge, which during the ages has been cutting its channel through the rock. Attention is directed to a telephone, and the guide advises that telephones throughout the Caverns are connected with the Lodge. Next one is astonished to see plant life so far underground. It made its appearance after the lighting installation and includes several species of mosses and liverwort. These tiny growths are pioneers and explorers of the plant world. Next, above the one hundred and fifty foot bridge which spans the chasm, is Juliet's Balcony, a lovely group of clustered tassels which have taken on an ivory tint. The sightseer then is awed by a massive Balanced Rock which seems to be lightly supported but has maintained its position for hundreds of centuries. Adjacent to the Balanced Rock is a stalactite resembling *a Hand of Tobacco* hung up to cure. Next is seen a vast terrace of stalactites, stalagmites, and flowstone, vari-colored from a light cream, up through shades of ivory into rich bronze. Other formations near this spot are the Fish Market, Flying Boat, Lighthouse, and Sentinels.

"The Rocky Mountains are an imposing pile of

rock, one of the wonders of this subterranean world. The space between the highest crag and the ceiling gives the effect of mountain scenery and a skyline. Below the level of the pathway the rocks are honeycombed with grottoes illumined with floods of crimson light which suggests the name, Dante's Inferno.

"Beyond the Rocky Mountains is the highest vaulted ceiling in the caverns, where the mechanical forces have worked through two periods of geological time. This, called the Temple of Titan, is a vast elliptical shaped chamber, fit dwelling place for Titan, the monster of mythology. At the entrance is a huge flowstone formation resembling a Turtle standing on its tail. Children like to imagine that it represents some mythological character transformed into this ungainly shape.

"The Chinese Pagoda is a cylindrical formation of beautiful ivory-tinted calcite. It is eleven feet, six inches high from the bed of the River Styx in which it stands, and nine feet, six inches in circumference near the base.

"The Tower of Pisa is a leaning cylinder of calcite with water-worn indentations. It recalls to mind the leaning tower under Italy's sunny skies.

"The Witch of the Grottoes is a profile in projecting rock of an ancient hag with bony features and jagged teeth. A second witch not quite so strikingly outlined leers over her shoulder.

"The Great Beehive is a stalagmite about twenty feet in height, which resembles on a mammoth scale the object for which it is named. The floor on which this unique formation once rested has been worn away by erosion so that the hive is nearly suspended.

"Titan's Fireplace is next viewed with an opening above insuring good draft. This is the 'flue'. Glowing embers are cunningly suggested by red lamps concealed so that only the color is visible. A little further on a stalagmite known as Huckleberry Finn's Hat amuses the observer, and a second giant Turtle "suns" himself. Both are in the bed of the River Styx.

"The visitor now approaches the natural island, passes the Inverted Village and Home of the Fairies. The Inverted Village shows a church steeple with a white cross, upside down; a barricade with a tower; and other oddly-shaped, small stalactites. The Home of the Fairies is a mass of colorful flowstone covering the side wall of the cavern below the inverted village. The cavern ceiling over the Pool of Siloam is a series of water-worn, curved arches which would do credit to a Phidias [a mythological sculptor]. These arches are extremely fascinating, but their charm is enhanced by the wonderful reflections in the pool. Near one end of the pool are ancient suncracks two hundred feet underground.

"Through the next passageway, called the Cathedral Archway, is seen the Pipe Organ, formed of large coalesced stalactites, which viewed in perspective resemble organ pipes of ivory hue, beautified with a rich, satiny sheen. An organ note is actually sounding, and can be traced to the overflowing waters of the lake far down the caverns. Opposite the pipe organ is an imposing formation known as the Bishop's Pulpit. The atmosphere is so truly ecclesiastical that one feels hushed and reverent."

Today one of the highlights of the tour, the underground

boat ride, wasn't ready for the caverns' opening in 1929. The two-ton flat-bottom boats, named Alcestis and Venus, were assembled in the cave in time for the 1930 tourist season.

A promotional flier, believed to have been written by Rickard, and printed prior to the caverns' grand reopening, described a mysterious (and provocative) "Lady of the Lake."

Rickard wrote:

"A stream flows through much of Howe Caverns, at one place forming a natural lake some 800 feet long, and in places 20 feet deep. And here is the 'Lady of the Lake', who, clothed in the habiliments of nudity, has, Lady Godiva-like, turned her face to the wall. No mortal who has traversed this passage has ever reported that the 'Lady' as even so much peeped over her shoulder."

The Lady of the Lake mysteriously disappeared sometime between the caverns' development and the launching of the Alcestis and Venus. The Lady was never made a part of the commercial tour.

A former tour guide who worked at the cave before the boats were added recalled Rickard pausing with his tour group at the head of the underground lake, making a dramatic appeal to the Lady to reveal herself. "And how are you today, m'lady?" he intoned.

"Why I'm just fine, Chauncey. And you?" answered caverns electrician Owen Wallace, who was working on the lake, just out of sight.

The underground boat ride is Howe Caverns' most heavily promoted feature and often its most memorable attraction. In *Story of Howe Caverns*, Clymer wrote of the boat ride: "The acoustics are such as to make even ordinary conversation musical and should one whistle, the reverberations turn the sound into a chorus of silvery flutes.

"It is easy to fancy one's self under a spell of complete enchantment."

Over the years, four boats have been added, and an orderly traffic schedule accommodates three tours in six boats at the same time on the narrow, one-eighth-mile underground lake.

In 1931, the General Electric Company presented the caverns a unique gift: an electric "moon," which was installed midway up the lake. (The caverns had purchased 24 miles of cable from GE to light the tourist route.) From total darkness, visitors would watch the round, yellow-lamp moon rise in the horizon, as colored lights became increasingly luminescent, controlled from the boat dock by the tour guide. Over the years, the moon became much battered by errant two-ton boats on the lake. It was discontinued in 1975 when the original caverns' lighting system was replaced.

Taped music, fed through two large speakers about midway up the Lake, replaced the moonrise. Until the tape became warped by humid cave conditions, boat passengers were entertained by a theme piece from Rodger and Hammerstein's "Victory at Sea," two hundred feet below the surface.

Resuming the trip on land, we return to Clymer's description from *Story of Howe Caverns*:

"Such formations are seen as the Giant Epaulet, Golden Cascade, Grottoes of the Naiads, Bottomless Pit, and the Kneeling Camel with its saddle bag. In a rock crevice back of the Bridal Altar is the exquisite little Lake of the Fairies, a shallow pool over which many tiny stalactites are forming. Small and delicate as they are, they were old when America was discovered, as the rate of growth of a stalagmite or stalactite is only about a cubic inch in a century.

"The Bridal Altar, in an impressive setting in the natural Balcony of Titan's Temple, is the romantic place where several marriages have been performed. At another spot, in 1854, Lester Howe's daughter was married, that being the first wedding in the Caverns. Looking up stream and down stream from the vantage point of the Balcony are two very beautiful underground vistas.

"Crossing the Rocky Mountains again, a Climbing Lizard, resembling the Gila Monster is seen. Along the walls of the Chasm, under the long bridge, beautiful effects are produced by electric lights. The beauty is greatly enhanced by the sheen on the chasm walls, dampened by the moisture from the rushing waters of the River Styx several feet below. Half way across the bridge is the Alcove of the Angels, a deep recess in the rocky walls, one of the most unusual spots in the Caverns. In it are stalactites, stalagmites, and flowstone, Nature's exquisitely beautiful stone handiwork in a variety of colorings from blue black and dark cream to pure white.

"The visitor now enters a unique and curious example of erosion by water called the Winding Way, a tortuous series of esses, about five hundred and fifty feet long, from three to six feet wide, and from ten to seventy-five feet high. The sightseer rounds curve after curve in bewildering succession, for the "Way" is so crooked that one seems to change his direction at each step. Much interest is expressed when it is learned that the bricks in the walk are laid lengthways north and south. The formations in the Winding Way show loveliness on a more delicate scale than elsewhere in the Caverns. Nature has sculpted two perfect rosebuds on the lower edge of a stalactite. A 'bit of eternal ice' called the Glacier is set like a keystone in a natural arch. It is the purest specimen of calcite found in the Caverns. The Kissing Bridge spans the passageway overhead. The Broken Idol is next, a pleasing calcite formation sometimes call Niobe, who in mythology became involved in a disastrous love affair and wept herself into stone.

"The visitor now enters the Silent Chamber. Here is Pluto's Niche. In order that one may experience the depths of silence and of darkness, the guide requests quiet for a moment and extinguishes all light. This is the final touch to the awe and wonderment of the pilgrimage. When the lights are turned on the Stained Glass Window is seen. Nature has colored it a beautiful old rose tint, with cross lines in diamond shapes. It is a solid block of calcite, approximately six inches thick and extends across the Winding Way about eight feet above the walk. The visitor ends his Caverns trip by retracing his steps through the Winding Way, and is carried to the surface in one of the near-by elevators.

"Back into the sunlight, the wonderful mountain and valley panorama seen from the Lodge is vested with new charm. The visitor always will retain awe-inspiring memories of this hidden marvel, wrought by the Great Architect of the Universe throughout eons and eons of Time."

Clymer concludes his description of the cave tour with an appropriate selection from the Bible:

"The words of the Psalmist (104:24) take on new meaning: 'O Lord, how manifold are thy works! In wisdom hast thou made them all: the earth is full of thy riches."

The stream of water that runs through Howe Caverns—the River Styx—continues to rise and fall according to outside conditions. Occasionally, the cave is closed because of flooding. There is no danger to tourists of being trapped by rising water, but several have gotten their feet wet over the years, in hasty retreat to the elevators.

In 1938, a tremendous flood washed out the original gravel walkways. The gravel was replaced by 88,000 bricks as a more permanent path through the cavern. The worst flood, in July 1976, filled the cave to the ceiling with water. The force of the water was so great that it ripped whole sections of brick from the caverns' man-made pathways.

Howe Caverns and its facilities will never be without electric power. Two large generators in the basement of the caverns' lodge supply backup power—enough to light a community of 2,500 homes.

There are few bats in the well-lit portions of Howe Caverns. Approximately one thousand brown bats live in the cave near the original entrance, which opens into the abandoned cement quarry.

"HOWE CAVERNS," in letters 10-feet high and of white cement, were placed on the hillside at the base of the entrance lodge in the late 1950s. For many travelers, this is their first impression of the cave as they approach from any of the roads that lead to Howe Caverns. It is probably the most frequently photographed portion of a visit to the famous cave.

Over the years, more than two hundred weddings have taken place in the caverns' new Bridal Altar. Permission and special arrangements can be made through the caverns' management.

Cave scenes for the 1972 television movie *Tom Sawyer* were filmed in Howe Caverns. The movie starred Josh Albee as Tom Sawyer and actors Buddy Ebsen and Jane Wyman, with Vic Morrow as Injun Joe. The movie also featured several Howe Caverns employees in bit parts in the cave scenes.

Nearly ten years ago, Howe Caverns, Inc. commemorated a business landmark: a fiftieth anniversary celebration held on June 1 and 2, 1979. Unique to the occasion was a reunion of the caverns' former guides, celebrating "50 Years of Guided Tours." Nearly two hundred returned to the site of their summer jobs to enjoy the catered affair. Those attending regaled each other with tall tales and amusing anecdotes, frequently at the expense of the touring public. Among the long-standing favorites: "Is this real air we're breathing?" "How many miles of unexplored cave are there?" "Is it dark down here at night?"

A program booklet was assembled, and letters of congratulations were solicited and began pouring in. A resolution honoring the cave guides' "enthusiasm and concern" when "encouraging . . . an appreciation of our nation's natural wonders" was received from the Carter administration's Secretary of Commerce, Juanita Kreps. Similar honoraria were presented by the New York State Assembly, and the Schoharie County Board of Supervisors.

Howe Caverns, Inc. recently celebrated its sixtieth anniversary, in 1989, with similar fanfare. It is likely that the caverns will continue to operate successfully into the distant future. In nearly a century and a half, Howe's Cave has captured the imagination of countless millions of visitors. Lester Howe's 1842 discovery took place at a time when the American public yearned to know more about their ever-expanding world and eagerly sought their country's natural wonders. Inspired by the early naturalists (whose ranks included popular literary figures, painters, and explorers), the mysteries revealed in Howe's Cave satisfied a growing public demand. In doing so, a profitable—if unusual—business was established, and a human drama begun.

Visitors to the cave of over a century ago endured hardships that few nature-loving travelers would today. Led by crude oil lanterns, the curiosity seekers of the nineteenth century spent hour upon hour in the cave. They emerged cold, wet, and caked with mud, and in most instances grateful for the novel experience.

Throughout the mid- to late-1800s, the caverns' beauty was greatly magnified; its size grossly exaggerated. It is likely that the myths surrounding Howe's Cave developed unintentionally, fed by a public need for the grandeur of nature. Scientific inquiries and methods were refined as the country got older; the natural beauty of the cave was lessened by this aging—in perception, but not in fact.

Those associated with the cave suffered as well. Lester Howe, discoverer and eager host to the scientific minds of his day, was victimized by individuals who represented the changing times. Coinciding with Howe's fall from grace in the public's mind was the embrace of the new symbol of American greatness, the aggressive giants of industry. Joseph Ramsey—politician, railroad tycoon, banker, cave owner and manufacturer of cement—was a respected and admired leader of the early industrial revolution in New York State.

The age of industry, represented by men like Ramsey, nearly destroyed Howe's magnificent cave by exploiting its resources for their utilitarian value in the building trades. Yet it was the same industrious spirit for innovation and technological advance that rescued the cave with modern engineering techniques unique to the early twentieth century.

Tourists—nearly 250,000 each year—still marvel at the caverns' beauty, but it's not easy to appreciate the human drama of the cave's 150-year history. There are countless stories behind the well-kept brick paths, attractive lighting, and comfortable stroll 200 feet below the surface of the earth. Many of the personalities—and some of the tall tales—associated with the long history of Howe's Cave have endured. Most notable of course is Lester Howe, the "eccentric genius," whose place in the annals of New York State and in the history of cave exploration is permanently assured. Stories of Lester's odd behavior continue to circulate, and ambitious cave explorers still search the hills of Schoharie County for the fabled Garden of Eden Cave, "bigger and better." The other families and individuals whose lives have affected, and been affected by, the caves are lesser known, and undeservedly so. The Ramseys, John Mosner, the Sagendorfs, the Mallerys, the VanNattens, Edward Rew, Arthur VanVoris, and Clay Perry, as well as countless others, have made the story of Howe Caverns the most unique in the history of American caves and cave exploring.